S.A.F.E.T.Y.™ is su
to the heart of what
lems, fear and stress. ~... you've identified the element
that is causing your distress, then you can come up with
a practical solution to fix it. Without the model you are
often stumbling around in the dark of your own emotions
and fear, with only a vague idea of the cause. Understanding what is causing your discomfort is powerful. Life
changes once you have that information. A most valuable
tool to add to your "surviving life" toolkit!

—**Debbie Jeremiah**, Former Faculty, GE Crotonville

The lessons in psychological safety are critical to building
and maintaining a creative culture of innovation. Creating
a "brain conscious" team with trust, fairness, autonomy,
and the other elements of the SAFETY model allows
people to take risks and see the possibilities that will drive
their organization to new heights. A must read for com-
panies and leaders looking to evolve and grow.

—**Jesse Meschuk**, SVP, Human Resources,
Blizzard Entertainment

For the last year and a half, Herman Miller has been
embarking on a journey to create a coaching culture
within our sales organization. There has been a significant effort to elevate the quality of conversations between
sales leaders and their teams using an applied neuroscience approach to coaching. At the core of this work is
understanding how to minimize threat in conversations
using ABL's SAFETY model. Our sales leaders are using
this model to begin conversations by addressing SAFETY
and then closely observing how to continually make sure
the brain's social needs are being met throughout the

interaction. What we have observed is that this creates a higher degree of engagement in the conversation (even difficult conversations) by both parties and a higher focus on creating conditions that allow us to work from the PFC instead of becoming hijacked by the amygdala, which results in better outcomes for all.

—**Heather Esposito**, Senior Manager, Global Leadership Development, Herman Miller

SAFETY rocks! We use the SAFETY drivers within our work team to understand each other and collaborate better. Plus we use SAFETY in our client projects to help us connect better with audiences and create more meaningful messages.

—**Jan Burnham**, CEO, ROC Group

I was introduced to SAFETY for improving leadership, management, and workplace culture. It challenged me to evaluate my own drivers, become more mindful of my reactions, and be more intentional about the way I approach others. I became more curious about the centrality of psychological safety across sectors and age-groups. It is the conceptual structure of this model that makes it universally accessible and having spent my career in the field of PreK-12 international education, I'm confident that SAFETY can transform workplace culture when integrated into educational contexts, as we prepare future generations to be mindful and motivated to make lasting contributions in their chosen field.

—**Phil Evans**, Development Specialist, International Baccalaureate

Understanding more about the brain and how it works can provide a significant and powerful underpinning to how we can change, how we do adapt, and how we can be more successful. We are now seeing application in the corporate environment that is different: people enjoying being at work, the organizations are thriving, more able to retain their people, less absenteeism, less turnover, able to attract better talent, the organization is able to be more innovative and create new ideas. When we see this happening and we see that the organization is more neurally aligned, then that is the evidence to say, why aren't we all doing this? We need to be more brain-friendly, we need to have awareness and tools that create awareness, so that we can behave in a more humane way—and it is also going to provide competitive advantage.

—**Carla Street**, Brain-based Leader Practitioner

SAFETY, and any other model, is only judged by its efficacy. The model and its delivery are world-class in delivering wisdom in the capsule of simplicity. In my experience with it in the work environment across various clients, it could not be more complex material (it is our brain after all …) delivered most elegantly with inspired energy. I find its scientific approach is intriguing to the technical folks, while the delivery is inviting to the emotional folks—everyone can access the wisdom—and isn't that the point? After that, the model is memorable, and therefore easier to deploy across a group faster. Since all we have is time, that ROI measures on the Richter scale.

—**Amit Kothari**, CEO, Kothari Leadership & Business Advisory

The greatest learning for me has been the role of the automated nonconscious brain in creating biases. SAFETY is a particularly useful approach and method to understand these nonconscious biases and how they shape our perspective of the world, our expectations and views. In a team environment it explains the differing responses within the group to the same stimuli. Establishing a team environment that enhances psychological safety provides advantages in realizing high performance, insightfulness, and innovation, three elements critical to organizational success.

—**Robert McKee**, Coach and Management Consultant

The SAFETY model is an innovative way to leverage brain science, enabling leaders to communicate and lead in a brain-friendly and effective manner.

—**Marcia Mueller**, VP, Global Leadership
Development, IMPACT Group

The human brain works in strange and wonderful ways, some of which are not always beneficial in helping us achieve our desired results. The SAFETY model clearly and concisely shows how we as individuals can understand the working of our own brains, and it enables us to use this understanding to help us improve our personal relationships. Just as significantly, it enables us to lead and work more effectively in project teams, an increasingly important vehicle in achieving business success.

—**Carl Belack**, Executive Coach and Complex
Project Consultant

This is essential information about our mind. I had no idea the factory settings for our brains were likely to cause problems, especially under stress in a leadership position.

—**Alex Vorobieff**, Business Consultant

PSYCHOLOGICAL SAFETY

PSYCHOLOGICAL SAFETY

The key to happy, high-performing people and teams

DAN RADECKI PHD, MA & LEONIE HULL
WITH JENNIFER MCCUSKER PHD & CHRISTOPHER ANCONA

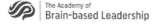

The Academy of
Brain-based Leadership

First published in 2018 by the Academy of Brain-based Leadership
Phone: +1 415 935 4027
Email: info@brainleadership.com
To learn more about the Academy of Brain-based Leadership, please visit
www.brainleadership.com

Produced by Sally Collings, Red Hill Publishing
Design by Tabitha Lahr
Edited by Sabine Sloley

ISBN: 978-1-7321595-0-1

10 9 8 7 6 5 4 3 2

To a new and higher way, to building bridges and breaking down walls

When will we make the same breakthroughs in the way we treat each other as we have made in technology?
—Theodore Zeldin (b. 1933), historian and author

CONTENTS

ACKNOWLEDGMENTS

Writing and producing this book would not have been possible without the significant contribution of content and support from an extraordinary group of people.

Our deep gratitude goes to all of you who have shared the load and helped bring this important work to life. Thank you for embracing our story, for believing in our vision and for sharing our passion to make a difference through this message.

—Dan Radecki & Leonie Hull

To Jennifer McCusker, whom we have to thank for challenging us and keeping us accountable, and continually reminding us of the importance and urgency of this book. Our sincere gratitude for your valuable contribution to the team context scenarios and the flavor and voice you brought to the book. We deeply appreciate your wisdom, your guidance, and your advocacy as an authentic practitioner and champion of this message. It is a joy collaborating with someone who shares our passion, not only for improving workplaces, but also for impacting the next generation.

Sincere gratitude goes to Chris Ancona for the many months spent critically reflecting and developing the S.A.F.E.T.Y.™ domain attributes and values, as well as your critical thought partnership and contribution to the product development of the SAFETY products. We deeply respect your commitment to data and debate, and to ensuring scientific alignment and integrity. Your personal sacrifice, sweat equity and investment into our mission, and your dedication to our success are humbling. Your friendship, loyalty, integrity, and drive to make a difference are deeply valued and cherished.

Thank you to Phil Dixon for your contribution to the S.A.F.E.T.Y.™ model and assessment and for working with us to get the Academy of Brain-based Leadership off the ground.

To Zach Brown, whose personal commitment and sacrifice helped us bring our message to the world. Thank you for untangling us when we were caught in the weeds, and for listening and sharing your insights as we grappled with finding our voice and story.

To two of our greatest supporters and encouragers, Judy Williams and Gemma Brown. Thank you for your tireless efforts to sustain us and keep the wheels turning, and for your companionship in the trenches on the ABL journey. Your loyalty and commitment to this work, and to us, matters more than you will ever know.

We are indebted to those who invested hours in reading and reviewing the draft manuscripts and designs and providing feedback: Zach Brown, Ellen Brown, Chris Ancona, Sally Collings, Sabine Sloley, Judy Williams, Craige Hull, Sara Radecki, Alexis Radecki, David Teagle, Donna Teagle, Lachlan Hull, Kath Teagle, Gemma Brown, Colin Brown, Paul Cushing, Caleb Brown, and Kelsey Brown.

To the professional production team who got us over the line and made the book a reality: Sally Collings, you were a godsend. Thank you to you and your team: Sabine Sloley, Tabitha Lahr, Dean Burrell, and Chris Hemesath.

Of course none of this would be possible without the support of our amazing families. Our deepest gratitude to Sara Radecki and Craige Hull, and to our kids, who continue to endure and support us and our vision. Thank you for your personal sacrifice, for standing alongside us and enabling us to do what we love. You continue to entertain our aspirations and ride the valleys and peaks; we wouldn't be here without you.

Finally, this book would not have been possible without the situations and people that have highlighted to us the critical nature of this message, and the importance of psychological safety in our lives and our workplaces. Sometimes it is in knowing what something isn't that you define what it is. As such some of our most important lessons and greatest inspirations for this work come from those places where psychological safety was not present. We have watched people, teams, and organizations thrive in contexts where it is nurtured, and experienced the collateral damage when it is neglected. It is these experiences that serve as critical reminders to us for why we do what we do; they inspire us and reinforce our commitment to this message.

Dear reader,

Right now, you don't know us, and we don't know you. So let's start off by depicting the ideal reader for this book, to set clear expectations from the outset.

Based on our research, the ideal reader for this book fits this profile:

1. Loves change and the challenge of the unknown, and thrives when pushed out of their comfort zone.
2. Takes pleasure in being compliant, and is excited about learning new rules, checklists, and metrics to implement in their daily routine.
3. Highly intelligent, ideally with a PhD-level education, and able to understand and apply complex neuroscientific principles.
4. Male, age 25–50, or female without children, age 30–45.

Yours sincerely,
The Academy of Brain-based Leadership

Insulted? Outraged? Irate?
OK ... now breathe and read on.

INTRODUCTION

After reading that letter, are you ready to tell us what we should do with our research and our book?

If so, perfect! It means we have succeeded in what we set out to do: to provoke strong thoughts and reactions. You may be experiencing physical sensations such as an elevated pulse, a churning in your stomach, or a clenching of your muscles. Or you may be feeling emotional responses such as anger, resignation, outrage, or rejection.

What you have just experienced is an attack to your psychological safety.

That description of our ideal reader is quite false. It is intended only to introduce you to the concept of psychological safety and what it feels like when that is threatened. In fact, before we move on, let's set the record straight. Only one criterion exists for reading this book—being human. This book is intended for everyone: the people in our families, our workplaces, our communities, and . . . our mirrors.

The exercise most likely triggered you on multiple levels. Some statements probably provoked more of a reaction than others, as we all have different sensitivities to what we perceive as threatening. Did you feel an attack to your self-esteem, your sense of belonging, your freedom, your sense of fairness, your certainty?

You might have found it difficult to continue reading or to concentrate. Perhaps you felt hijacked by a flood of thoughts and emotions that made you feel disenfranchised, alienated, marginalized, hopeless, or rejected, or that you perceived as unfair, condescending, arrogant, or rude.

Feeling psychologically threatened is a negative experience that disrupts and derails thinking and emotions, damages relationships, impacts productivity, and damages health. We encounter these small stings to various degrees all day, every day, inflicted either by us or on us. Mostly, they fall below our level of consciousness.

What Is Psychological Safety?

Most of us understand the importance of physical safety. We protect ourselves and those around us. For example, we typically learn at a young age that hitting someone with our fists when we are angry is socially unacceptable and not conducive to sustaining healthy relationships or personal well-being. Well-defined parameters exist for classifying physical interactions as socially acceptable, helpful, or harmful.

Psychological safety, however, is a new frontier. Only now are we beginning to understand its importance and impact, thanks to recent advancements in neuroscience. For example, research shows that a "hit" to our psychological safety can have a deeper and longer-lasting impact than a "hit" to our physical selves. In fact, social rejection has the same impact on the brain as a punch to the face

(Eisenberger, 2012). Over time, the pain associated with a physical attack is difficult or impossible to recall. The memory of social rejection, however, even many years after the fact, can elicit the same strength of emotion as it did at the time of the event.

When we experience an attack to our psychological safety, like the example given in the introduction, our brain is triggered into a stress response. Our cognitive abilities are compromised. Our higher, logical brain, the one responsible for thinking, creativity, decision-making, and self-control, goes off-line. In this derailed stress state we can find it difficult to concentrate, make decisions, or control our emotions (Lupien, 2012). Maintaining psychological safety is an important factor for optimizing our performance and well-being.

Why Is It Relevant Now?

Until recent years, very little scientific knowledge existed about the detrimental impact to the brain when psychological safety is compromised. Although there were many theories about the brain, essentially it remained a mystery. Most of what we did know was based on observations of the functioning and behavior of people with damage to particular areas of their brains, through accidents or defects.

This began to change about 27 years ago with the invention of functional Magnetic Resonance Imaging (fMRI). The functional MRI measures brain activity during a specific task and time period, as opposed to the static MRI most often used to diagnose brain (and other tissue) disorders. This technological evolution has put the brain front and center, making it a focus of fascination and research. We learned more about the brain in the last three decades than we did in all of prior history.

For the first time we were able to observe and measure the brain in action, opening the doors to a better understanding of what motivates us, what drives us, what threatens us, and how we deal with the world around us, not just on the basis of personal perception and observation of behavior, but from the perspective of the physical activity and physiological processes in our brains.

Research, performed in both the scientific and industry arenas, suggests that paying close attention to psychological safety has tangible benefits, not just to personal health and well-being, but to workplace productivity and performance. That bears repeating:

Psychological safety has been identified as a critical factor for effective work teams (Duhigg, 2016).

Amy Edmondson at Harvard defines psychological safety in the team context as *"a belief that one will not be punished or humiliated for speaking up with ideas, questions, concerns, or mistakes, and that the team is safe for interpersonal risk taking."* (Edmondson, 1999)

Psychological safety gained increased attention when the findings from some compelling research conducted by Google (the Aristotle Project) were published in 2015. In its quest to build the perfect team, Google assessed the factors common to their high-performing teams. They looked at over a hundred teams within their company over the period of a few years and were shocked to find it was not the background, the experience, or the education of the team members that determined the team's success, but whether psychological safety was present within the team (Duhigg, 2016).

In a psychologically safe climate, team members are not afraid to express themselves; they feel accepted and respected. This openness creates a fertile environment for thinking, creativity, innovation, and growth, and leads to more collaborative relationships and an overall improvement in team productivity.

Edmondson identified that psychological safety was most critical for teams with interdependent members and in times of uncertainty. In our experience, that covers the majority of functioning teams.

So, if harming psychological safety is so damaging, and the benefits of protecting psychological safety are so great, why don't we give it the same attention in society as we do physical safety?

A New Approach to Safety

Hopefully by now you are convinced of the merits of psychological safety. But how do you practice it? How can you implement it in your life and your workplace to reap the benefits of increased productivity and personal well-being?

Let us introduce you to the S.A.F.E.T.Y.™ model. Based on neuroscience research, the model describes some of the most important social motivators of human behavior. We will dive into the details of each of these drivers later in the book. For now, the overview on the next page will suffice.

The model will not only help you understand how you are driven, and how you derive your psychological safety, but also help you become aware of these factors in the people around you. Our aim is to create "brain-conscious" cultures by providing the knowledge and tools for people to protect their own psychological safety, and that of others. We tackle this goal one brain at a time—through self-awareness.

Once you have built awareness, you will be empowered to defuse, sidestep, and reframe conflict in order to be your best self and your best team player.

THE S.A.F.E.T.Y.™ MODEL

SECURITY
Our need for predictability:
- Consistency
- Commitment
- Certainty
- (No) Change

YOU
Factors unique to 'you':
- Your personality profile
- Your biases
- How you are influenced
- Your context (past, present, future)

AUTONOMY
Our need to feel we have control over our environment, and have choices

TRUST
Our social need to belong to and protect our 'in-group'

FAIRNESS
Our need to engage in and experience fair exchanges, both to us and to others

ESTEEM
Our need to be regarded highly, derived by how we:
- See ourselves
- Compare ourselves to others
- Think others see us

UNDERSTANDING YOUR BRAIN

Some of the brain's core principles operate at a noncon-scious level. Before jumping into the specific drivers of psychological safety, you may find it helpful to understand how this mysterious organ protects us, but also, quite often, sabotages us.

You Are Wired for Safety

Over the past two million years, the human brain has evolved to maximize our chances of surviving. The best way it found to do this was to wire itself for safety above all else. The trials and errors of tribal life educated the brain not only on which behaviors created winning outcomes and enhanced survival probability, but also on situations and behaviors that man-dated caution, or presented all-out threats.

For example, roaming alone in the jungle armed with only a pebble and a stick was probably not going to work out too well when you came face-to-face with a saber-toothed tiger. If by chance you did manage to escape, you were unlikely to repeat that adventure. Unfortunately, it is more likely that your error of judgment put an end to you and your contribution to the human gene pool, but it would have provided a valuable lesson to the tribe.

The brain is essentially a big prediction machine designed to establish patterns from our experiences, map them, and then hardwire them as blueprints for living to keep us safe.

Furthermore, the brain is wired to place great importance on establishing, securing, and maintaining bonds with others (i.e., our "social" brain), because in those early years that was the most efficient way to ensure survival (Dunbar, 1998).

These hardwired blueprints created specific motivations and behaviors to sustain individuals and their tribes over time. They continue to impact you today: how you think, how you behave, how you are motivated, and how you derive your psychological safety.

Your brain's drive for safety is so important that it has developed many more networks to monitor, detect, and manage threat than it has created pathways for rewards (Gordon, 2013). Threat-related brain networks react faster, stronger, and for a longer period of time than reward networks. (Think of your reaction to an insult versus a compliment.) Unless you feel safe, it's very difficult to focus on or enjoy anything.

Much of this is driven by a part of your brain called the amygdala. From an evolutionary standpoint, the amygdala has been around for a long time. Although it is small, it has well-established neural pathways to drive nonconscious behavior. It is responsible for processing emotion and reacting to fear or threat. It drives the primal "fight or flight" response. The amygdala evolved to be extremely efficient. Pattern recognition and threat detection carry on continuously, without your awareness. We call this a "negativity bias." At a nonconscious level, you tend to focus on threat and danger above everything else.

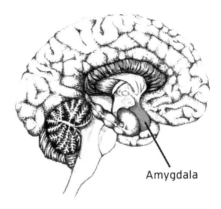

Amygdala

While this ancient brain system is essential, and has been responsible for the success of the human species, it can be argued that what it perceives as threat and how it reacts to those threats has become inappropriate and irrational in today's relatively "safe" society.

Indeed, society has evolved to a point where, for many of us, worries about moment-to-moment survival are a distant memory. From your brain's perspective, however, the fundamental challenges of survival are still very much relevant, leaving you with a society and way of life that is at odds with the way your brain is biologically wired.

The negativity bias, which was designed to keep you safe, now attributes danger and threat to relatively harmless situations, like being overwhelmed by email, squeezed by looming deadlines, juggling conflicting priorities, or meeting new people. These are far from the deadly threats your tribal ancestors faced, things like starvation, or attack by a neighboring tribe, or the risk of being devoured by wild animals.

Unfortunately, your brain doesn't know the difference. It treats your everyday, benign threats the same way it would treat an attack by a mastodon, triggering you into a psychologically unsafe state and driving inappropriate reactions and behaviors.

YOUR BRAIN'S SAFETY NEEDS

Your brain is hardwired for safety and has not evolved at the same pace as society. From a perspective of psychological safety, this means:

- At a nonconscious level you are preoccupied with safety.
- You have a negativity bias that tends to focus on threat and danger above everything else.
- Your brain perceives and responds to psychological threats the same way it does physical threats.

You Are on Autopilot

So why do you fall victim to this irrational process?

Your brain deals with an estimated 11 million bits of information per second, each and every day. This would be impossible if it didn't use highly efficient systems. Your brain relies heavily on automated, nonconscious processing, because dealing consciously with the bombardment of input from your world would be unmanageable. It is estimated that your brain manages over 99 percent of its input in a completely automated way, below your level of consciousness (Wilson, 2002).

The price of this efficiency is that you are on "automatic pilot" most of the time. Your nonconscious processes analyze information and automate your responses without your active thought or awareness. The mental shortcuts provided by your automatic brain can lead to decision or reaction biases. These may be as innocuous as a color or food preference, or have more serious implications, such as racial profiling.

For example, if you were raised in a town with no ethnic diversity, you may have a bias towards your cultural background and see anyone outside of that background as "different" and hence possibly dangerous.

YOUR AUTOMATED BRAIN

Your biases, created from your past experiences, are the invisible filters through which you see and engage with the world. From a psychological safety perspective, these nonconscious biases can:

- determine what you perceive as a threat, which can often be unwarranted, and
- automate your responses, which can often be irrational and inappropriate.

You Have a Copilot

So how do you stop being a victim of your biases?

Fortunately, as a human, you can mitigate your biases with the help of an evolutionarily "new" part of the brain called the prefrontal cortex or PFC.

Compared to the amygdala, the PFC is a part of our brain that came about later in our evolution. The PFC

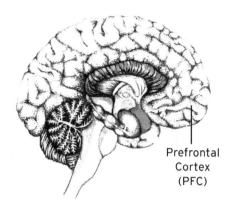

Prefrontal
Cortex
(PFC)

isn't typically fully developed in humans until we reach our early- to mid-twenties, making it the last part of the brain to fully mature. The PFC is engaged for conscious and logical thinking processes. It handles the executive elements that make you uniquely human, such as thinking and planning, being creative, displaying willpower, feeling empathetic, etc. (Arnsten, 2009).

When engaged effectively, the PFC allows you to manage the amygdala's automated biases and threat responses. The relationship between these two brain regions is like a typical good vs. evil story, with the amygdala representing the old and powerful "dark side," and the PFC acting as the younger, emerging hero who strives for a greater good and fights to control the dark force's dominion over your behavior. It's a constant battle for your higher brain (PFC) to keep a lid on your lower brain's (amygdala's) threat response.

You have no doubt experienced a moment when you've become frustrated with a person or a situation. Sometimes the frustration can be so great that you feel compelled to physically hit something, but, knowing it may not be socially acceptable, you (hopefully) choose to restrain yourself. This ability to pause before an action and engage self-control is directed by a specific part of the PFC known as the ventrolateral prefrontal cortex (VLPFC), or the region referred to as the "braking system."

Just as a brake on a car stops it from going out of control down a hill, the brain's braking system inhibits basic instincts instigated by the amygdala as part of your emotional response to a stimulus (Lieberman, 2013). This includes everything from deciding not to hit someone, to resisting the urge to eat a dozen donuts when on a diet, or putting your own opinion aside and listening to another's perspective during an argument or discussion.

Since the PFC is a relatively "new" part of the brain, it is much slower and not nearly as efficient as your nonconscious brain at processing what's happening in your world. It doesn't operate with the same strength and quickness as does the amygdala. Your PFC also requires a tremendous amount of resources (oxygen and glucose) to operate effectively and enable you to "brake" any unwanted behavior. Therefore, if you use it too much over a short period, the PFC will fatigue, start to slow, and eventually shut down.

Chances are you experience this on a regular basis. It happens whenever you lose focus at school during a class in which you work through stressful exercises, or at the office after a long meeting that required you to make a lot of decisions. You may notice in those moments that you become agitated by small distractions or minor annoyances, or are much less productive. Your PFC has been drained and needs to restore.

A good way to picture PFC fatigue is to observe a small child becoming frustrated. If you take a toy away from a baby, that child will become emotional, cry, and lash out. This is partially because that baby doesn't have a fully formed PFC. What you're seeing is the inability to manage basic emotion. In extreme cases, pushing yourself too hard through an exhausted PFC can lead to a state of total burnout in which you shut down your ability to function properly.

On the other hand, the sophistication of the human PFC gives you the unique advantage over other species to think logically and analytically, be creative, self-regulate, empathize, and take perspective. It is your tool for overcoming the instinctive behavior that your "old brain" wants to impose on you.

YOUR BRAKING SYSTEM

Your PFC is largely responsible for determining your effectiveness and productivity. From a psychological safety perspective, the PFC:

- has the ability to brake our automated brain's threat triggers, and
- can use rationality and logic to override our innate nonconscious impulses and reactions when psychologically threatened.

Your Daily Grind

So how do you keep your vulnerable PFC in the driver's seat and at optimal performance?

Let's talk about stress . . .

We have all heard the warnings about the negative health impacts of stress. Indeed, stress is becoming an epidemic in our fast-paced and constantly changing world. The bad press is warranted, as the damaging effects of excessive stress on both your physical health and your brain health are real.

Recent breakthroughs in neuroscience research are exposing serious consequences for the chronically stressed brain. Due to the vulnerability of the PFC, chronic stress can actually cause it to physically change and weaken (Arnsten, 2012). When this happens, a person may experience "amygdala hijack," which includes cognitive slowing, emotional outbursts, and the inability to use the PFC's braking system.

To make matters worse, prolonged stress can cause the amygdala to grow in size and strength (Arnsten, 2012). This tips the scales further in favor of the already strong nonconscious processes, kicking you out of the driver's seat and allowing the autopilot to take over.

Research suggests that, over a long period of stress, these physical brain changes can extend to other higher brain areas and contribute to memory loss, and possibly even dementia and Alzheimer's (Mah, 2016). Therefore, managing your stress levels is critical to your behavior and well-being.

If you have suffered from, or are currently suffering from, chronic stress, please know that there is light at the end of the tunnel. The brain is, by design, a wonderfully adaptive organ, and the physical impacts on the brain from stress can be reversed by employing stress management strategies.

So if your goal is to stay in the "conscious" driver's seat and keep your PFC online, the research suggests that stress is your enemy—right?

Not so fast.

It may come as a surprise that this is not the whole story regarding stress and the brain. A certain, optimal, amount of stress (arousal) is important to maintain the brain's peak performance.

We see this in the "Optimal Arousal Curve." (Cools, 2015)

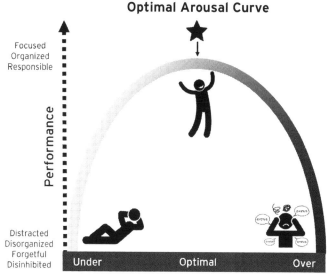

Adapted from Dr Amy F T Arnsten, Yale School of Medicine

You'll notice that this curve is shaped like an inverted U. The top of the curve represents the ideal amount of stress (or emotional arousal) necessary for us to be organized, creative, and efficient. However, after a certain point, too much stress (or overarousal) will push you "over the edge," impacting your PFC and causing you to lose focus, become less productive, and start reacting emotionally.

At the other extreme, not enough stress (underarousal) can leave you completely unmotivated to act and can be as detrimental to your performance as overarousal.

Think of stress as fuel: too little and the PFC doesn't start, too much and stress floods the engine. In fact, the PFC is so demanding in its needs that it's been called the Goldilocks of the brain because it needs everything to be "just right" . . . the right amount of glucose, the right amount of oxygen, the right amount of stimulation, etc.

The Optimal Arousal Curve is a useful tool for understanding why stress impacts different people in different ways. It is important to note that not everyone requires the same level of stress to reach their optimal level.

Consider for a moment that you are someone (Person A) whose resting state is at the left end of this curve. You may need quite a bit more stress (arousal) to get you to that "sweet spot" where your PFC is firing on all cylinders. This is sometimes known as being "in the zone" or in the "flow state." Those who identify as being on the left of the curve may have a tendency to leave things to the last minute before they kick into action, using the rush or pressure of a time constraint to help them focus on getting the job done.

Alternatively, suppose you normally fall somewhere in the middle of the curve (Person B). You may already intrinsically have what you need to be motivated, and any additional arousal may push you over the edge toward "burnout."

Now imagine a work-team social event. Invitees from Group B (those who identify with having a resting state of "middle" on the Optimal Arousal Curve) are likely to be people who avoid a lot of external attention. This group does not usually seek out large-scale social activities and may either not turn up or, if they feel compelled to attend, will be the ones standing awkwardly by the exit.

People from Group A, on the other hand, may seek out settings where they receive a lot of external focus. They are often described as "the life of the party." These individuals are likely to put in a 60-hour workweek or, at the extreme, swim with sharks. The higher stress level makes them feel like they are "in the zone."

Brain Safety N.E.T.S.™

Let's briefly talk about how you can set yourself up to be less impacted by stress and threat. From a physiological, top-down perspective, if you maintain your PFC in optimal condition, it is far more likely to stay in the driver's seat and keep its hands on the wheel, avoiding the derailment of an "amygdala hijack" when you are psychologically threatened.

The approach is similar to building a muscle. Your goal is to strengthen the PFC and increase its capacity to control the amygdala and handle stress.

The brain likes to keep things simple when learning new material, so we will use the acronym N.E.T.S.™ to summarize the most important ways of keeping your PFC strong. NETS stands for Nutrition, Exercise, Training, and Sleep, all key components of PFC health. Think of how a safety net protects a trapeze artist during those amazing aerial stunts. The net is put in place proactively to manage injury in case of a fall.

In much the same way, building brain resilience pro-actively by managing our nutrition, exercise, training, and sleep can help us protect against the damage that can happen in our brains during stress (Tabibnia and Radecki, 2018).

The neuroscience of stress and resilience is a fascinating topic. The research into NETS and its implications offers critical insights for a world suffering from a stress epidemic. For now, we will merely touch on each of these components in the context of psychological safety, and discuss some practical ways for you to strengthen your PFC and build your capacity for resilience.

NUTRITION

Nutrition is an important piece of the puzzle when we talk about managing the brain and keeping it firing on all cylinders. There's good evidence that eating foods with the right "good" fats and focusing on a diet rich in anti-oxidants and vegetables can benefit the immune system and therefore benefit your brain's resilience (Zamro-ziewicz, 2016). But the concept of intermittent fasting is also an interesting topic in this nutrition bucket, with some sound science supporting it (Longo, 2013; Mattson, 2002).

The brain evolved over the course of millions of years, and for the vast majority of that time we lived moment to moment. We didn't have access to fast food or even regular meals. Not finding food meant certain death. Our brain evolved to be very focused when we were in starvation mode. Our ancestors needed to have their wits about them to find food. Research suggests that this mechanism still functions as it did thousands of years ago.

After we've gone about 16 hours without any calories, a sort of "switch" gets flipped in our brains to increase natural chemicals that make it a more efficient machine. These substances, known as growth factors, act like your brain's personal housekeeper, cleaning up debris and recycling anything needed for future activity (Marosi, 2014). When you consider that your brain has about 85 billion neurons with thousands of connections to each of those, it's easy to see why housekeeping is critical.

Studies are pointing to this housekeeping component as a way to prevent Alzheimer's, Parkinson's, age-related memory loss, and even cancer, so it's obviously important to keep a clean brain (Weinstein, 2014). An added benefit of increasing growth factors in the brain is that they seem to act as natural antidepressants. In fact, we think that many of the antidepressant drugs on the market these days work by artificially increasing brain growth factors.

The brain is a remarkably adaptable machine, and this mechanism can work to our advantage. Once your brain realizes that you haven't had any food for about 16 hours (possibly 12 hours in women), it activates the fasting switch and makes you more focused and mentally on top of your game.

EXERCISE

Another way to counteract some of the limitations of the PFC is with exercise. Recent research is showing the importance of regular exercise and its protective effect on the brain, particularly during times of stress (Nokia, 2016). The brain, especially the PFC, has naturally occurring chemicals that protect it from damage and allow it to repair itself. These chemicals become depleted during prolonged stress. Exercise seems to increase the availability of these protective chemicals so that our brain is more "resilient," enabling our braking system to operate longer and stronger. A stronger braking system is a huge asset when it comes to managing your threat response and dealing with some of your nonconscious negative biases.

TRAINING

Training in the NETS context refers to brain training.

A growing body of research supports the practice of simple, daily, focused meditation, or mindfulness. For example, recent findings suggest that mindfulness training can reverse the impact of stress on the brain. Such training has been shown to increase the efficiency of the PFC and decrease the strength of the amygdala (Holzel, 2010).

In the behavioral realm, a mindful state has been shown to decrease burnout, depression, and anxiety, while increasing sleep quality and job satisfaction (Krasner, 2009; Hulsheger, 2012). In addition, a fascinating study found that subjects who followed a mindfulness training program actually increased the protective proteins in their immune systems (Jacobs, 2011).

Focused brain training is gaining attention as a way to improve higher brain (PFC) functioning. It targets specific brain functions to strengthen or rewire networks and build brain capacity. Research over the past several years suggests that regular computerized brain training may be associated with measurable improvements in cognitive and emotional well-being, as well as increased efficiency in the braking system (Berkman, 2014).

While this field of brain training is in its infancy, the implications of being able to directly strengthen our higher brain networks with focused brain training, much like a muscle responding to weight lifting, is an exciting possibility.

SLEEP

Finally, sleep is another factor being researched with regard to building brain resilience. We need REM sleep, or dreaming, to give our brain a chance to deal with the millions of bits of information that bombarded it during the course of the day (Payne, 2016).

Research in rats has shown that neural networks activated during a learning task (e.g. how to navigate a maze for a reward) become active again when the rats are asleep that night. It's almost as if the brain replays the process over and over so that the information can be retained long term (Dudai, 2015).

Dreaming seems to be a way of prioritizing what was important, and hence what we need to remember in our long-term storage. Research is showing that impaired REM sleep can have a negative impact on our brain's ability to manage stress (Mellman, 2007). Generally, most adults need about seven hours of restful sleep per night to counteract the effects of stress.

BUILDING YOUR BRAIN FITNESS

1. You can minimize the impact of stress and keep a lid on the amygdala's stress response by strengthening your PFC's braking system and building your brain's resilience.
2. Resilience can be built using nutrition, exercise, training, and sleep.

KNOW YOUR BRAIN: SUMMARY

1. You are Wired for Safety: Your brain's primary focus is to detect and react to threats to your survival. It treats tangible physical threats and perceived psychological threats identically.

2. You Are on Autopilot: Your brain recognizes and hardwires patterns, and creates mental shortcuts (biases) to maximize efficiency, increase predictability, and protect your safety. Because this happens below the level of consciousness, you are on autopilot 99.9 percent of the time and are susceptible to nonconsciously attributing "threat" where it is not warranted, and reacting irrationally or inappropriately as a result.

3. You Have a Copilot: As humans we have evolved a unique, logical, higher brain, the PFC, that allows you to put the brakes on your automated brain and override your emotional, threat-focused, nonconscious processes. The PFC's resources are depleted with use, reducing its effectiveness over time. Managing its limitations is important.

4. Managing Your Daily Grind: Maintaining an optimal stress level can keep your PFC online and in the zone of peak performance. However, when you experience too much or too little stress, your performance is negatively impacted and you can become less focused, less productive, and susceptible to your automatic impulses.

5. Brain Safety N.E.T.S.™: Staying planted in the driver's seat and not being derailed by your automatic brain is a delicate balance. Your best chance at staying alert and optimizing your performance is to strengthen the capacity and function of your PFC and braking systems by being attentive to Nutrition, Exercise, brain Training, and Sleep.

THE S.A.F.E.T.Y.™ MODEL

By now we have established that your brain is preoccupied with your safety and survival. It has preset conditions, or biases, that it has hardwired as safety checks to minimize threat and maximize reward. It uses these automated mental "checklists," or biases, to categorize things as "bad" (threatening), or "good" (rewarding).

In a world where there is less threat to your physical safety than in prehistoric times, these biases, or filters, have become sensitive to the psychological threats you experience in your social interactions, things like attitudes, behaviors, and perceived motivations.

We now get to the core of psychological safety by looking at the bottom-up approach—how do you identify and manage the triggers that threaten your psychological safety and hijack your brain?

Social cognitive neuroscience is an emerging field of study that seeks to understand how our brain deals with information related to our behavior when interacting with others. Recent findings illustrate the critical importance of our social brain, showing that connecting with others is as fundamental to humans as the need for food or shelter.

Key research in this area was conducted by scientists at UCLA (Eisenberger, 2012). In one well-known experiment, a subject's brain activity was monitored in situations of social rejection—they perceived that they were being excluded during a game of virtual "catch" with other participants. The study found that the brain experiences social pain in the same way as physical pain. Social rejection is processed like physical threat.

If we look back to the times of tribal living, it stands to reason that social rejection would have been as detrimental to survival as physical threat. Consider the rule-breaker who was excluded from the tribe and cast out into the wilderness where his isolation left him exposed to the elements, to predators, and to starvation. The tribe provided security and resources, and we were safer and more effective in packs than we were by ourselves.

Given that social connection is such a fundamental human need, you'd think that we would have honed our ability to connect with everyone we meet. However, as a result of our complex human condition, we often act against our own self-interest when we experience situations that "threaten" our safety. Such situations can trigger insecurities that are expressed through shyness, self-consciousness, cynicism, pride, competitiveness, jealousy, or arrogance.

For example, you might not speak up to share your knowledge and expertise in a team strategy session because you feel intellectually inferior or are afraid your ideas will be rejected.

By understanding some of the basic social drivers that govern these behaviors, you can begin to identify your triggers and manage your reactions, as well as understand others' triggers and reactions.

S.A.F.E.T.Y.™ is a model that describes some of the important social factors that can trigger the powerful threat response in our brain and cause us to feel psychologically unsafe. We can think of these SAFETY domains as biases we use in our social contexts.

S.A.F.E.T.Y.™ stands for:

SECURITY

Our need for predictability:
- Consistency
- Commitment
- Certainty
- (No) Change

YOU

Factors unique to 'you':
- Your personality profile
- Your biases
- How you are influenced
- Your context
  (past, present, future)

AUTONOMY

Our need to feel we have control over our environment, and have choices

TRUST

Our social need to belong to and protect our 'in-group'

FAIRNESS

Our need to engage in and experience fair exchanges, both to us and to others

ESTEEM

Our need to be regarded highly, derived by how we:
- See ourselves
- Compare ourselves to others
- Think others see us

In the following section, we dig into the details of these SAFETY domains and demonstrate the research that supports the importance of these social triggers.

We will then introduce you to ten team members who personify the high need and low need of each domain. They will share their perspective on their strengths and challenges to help you gain insight into how they experience and react to the world. Although these personalities are depicted as extreme versions of the specific domain sensitivities, the emphasis will allow you to appreciate the unique attributes they bring to the table.

By immersing yourself in their experience, you will be better able to understand and respect their SAFETY needs. You will learn how to partner with them to best leverage their contribution while keeping them psychologically safe.

SECURITY

Security is the brain's need for predictability. Security is chunked into four "Big Cs": **C**onsistency, **C**ommitment, **C**ertainty, and the brain's general dislike of **C**hange.

The brain is essentially a big prediction machine. When the brain feels oriented, it feels safe. We want the people in our lives to be consistent. We want our environments and workplaces to stay consistent. In fact, we strive for our own behavior to be consistent, because we feel better when it is. Environments that are consistent and predictable are easier to navigate.

We can relax and don't need to think as much or engage the higher brain (PFC) as much to work out what's going on. In contrast, environments of change activate our brain's threat system when our lower brain (amygdala) responds to the stress created by uncertainty (Davis, 2016). So, what does "change" actually mean?

For each topic or concept that you need to understand and handle in life, your brain builds a map based on previous experience and exposure to the stimuli. These maps are the most efficient way for your brain to align what you see to a known concept. For example, you have probably created the concept of "tree" because you've built a picture of what you know and mean by "tree." It is tall, sturdy, has deep roots, and so on.

When new information arrives, the brain attempts to connect that information to an existing map. For example, when you learn that trees also have a system for transforming sunlight into energy, you include this information into your neural map of a tree. If the knowledge conforms to your existing map, it is integrated, and the reward system of your brain is activated.

This all happens very quickly and consumes little energy. The fact that a tree can generate energy via sunlight makes sense based on what you knew previously about its roots and leaves, so all is well with your sense of certainty about a tree, and your brain is happy.

However, if the new information does not align with your existing map, or is ambiguous, it will activate your threat circuitry. The degree to which our threat circuitry is activated differs for each of us. Think about the principle of moderation implied from the Optimal Arousal Curve we saw earlier. Although your brain does crave predictability, it also likes some novelty (albeit in small doses). The amount of novelty that you can tolerate depends on your current level of stress.

Returning to our tree example, if you now see a tree intentionally moving its branches to attack you, your brain would be confused. This does not align with your map of a tree, and would trigger a threat response as your brain deals with the fear of this new, uncertain, and unpredictable situation. Think of how enchanted forests are depicted in fairy tales to create a sense of suspense and anxiety.

New research shows that uncertainty causes our brain to perceive a neutral situation (neither bad nor good) as negative. In other words, uncertainty creates a negativity bias.

It is important to remember that no two brains are alike. The degree to which we can either tolerate or embrace change is different for all of us. The Optimal Arousal Curve implies that our sensitivity to stress depends on where we sit on the curve. For some, the stress caused by the novelty of change can be a motivator. If this is you, you may actually enjoy uncertainty, and even thrive in times of significant change.

Others are negatively impacted and triggered into a threat state by even the tiniest of changes. Consider the staff member who freaks out when they are forced to take a different position at the table in the meeting because someone has taken her usual seat, or who has a lot to say about the new brand of coffee in the break room.

If you know you have a low tolerance for inconsistency and unpredictability, then you know that these circumstances will trigger a threat state in your brain. Under this distress, you will have a tougher time remaining focused, reaching clear decisions, and keeping your higher brain (PFC) in control of your lower brain (amygdala). As a result, you might resist new ideas from others, or reject new opportunities that have implications for you and your routine.

Alternatively, if you have a high tolerance for change (i.e. a low sensitivity to security) you may unknowingly introduce change on a frequent basis to your family, friends, and teams, not realizing the negative impact it might have on them.

Now think about how this could impact your effectiveness.

SECURITY

Summary

- Security is the brain's need for predictability.
- The higher brain can be seen as a big prediction machine, always wanting to ensure that things in our world are familiar.
- Change is threatening to the brain, which craves consistency, commitment, and certainty, and dislikes change.
- Security makes the brain feel that its environment is safe. A lack of security leads to a negativity bias.

Stop now and consider . . .

1. How important is it to you that life be predictable and consistent?
2. How do you react to things that are inconsistent, change frequently, or are unpredictable?

SAM
High Security Need

Strengths
"I consider myself a loyal, stable, and dependable influence on the team. I'm great at keeping track of deliverables, following through on commitments, and creating order out of chaos. You can depend on me to take care of the details and to have all bases covered. I like to make sure we have policies and procedures to provide guidance and consistency in our work. I am often the necessary 'voice of reason' when evaluating new ideas or impending change, and have a knack for identifying potential associated risks."

Challenges
"I know I can be resistant to new thinking and ideas at times, and have been told that this can stifle the team's innovation and growth. I'm highly risk averse, which can sometimes sabotage my own or the team's success by not embracing and leveraging new opportunities. I sometimes need to be reminded and challenged to lift my thinking up out of the minutiae to avoid stagnating progress. I know some see my need for reassurance about my performance as a lack of confidence in my own ability. Some have reported feeling micromanaged when I monitor and track progress on their commitments and deliverables."

"Under times of stress, or when I'm highly triggered, I can become very prescriptive with an increased need for detail, compliance, and reassurance. I know I can become closed-minded and stubborn in my efforts to resist change. I feel safe when I feel certain about my world, so I'm nonconsciously driven to find ways to increase my sense of certainty, consistency, and clarity, and to avoid change in times of stress."

Management
To support my psychological safety and get the best from me:
- Be sure to keep your promises.
- Provide me with detail maps, e.g. processes and procedures.
- Overcommunicate and give details about expectations and potential risks.
- Allow space for me to ask lots of questions.
- Don't overwhelm me with too many changes at once.

SETH
Low Security Need

Strengths
"I am a great visionary, always pushing the team forward. I am constantly exploring new and improved processes and am the creative force driving us toward innovation and change. I don't shy away from risk. I see it as a challenge, and I'm happy to lead the way into uncharted territories. I see failure as a growth opportunity, and I recover and move on from my mistakes quickly."

Challenges
"I know my drive toward novelty and change can sometimes disrupt team stability. I know in my quest for chasing the 'next thing' I can lack follow-through on existing commitments and lose motivation and focus on projects that have lost their 'shine.' My low need for clarity or certainty means I am not sensitive to that need in others and I can be remiss in providing the attention to detail and direction they seek,

or leave people in a state of ambiguity for longer than they are comfortable with.

"Under times of stress, or in situations void of sufficient novelty and change, I tend to become apathetic and unmotivated. I have noticed I will disengage and find ways to escape, or conversely I will stir things up and become a disruptor or troublemaker in order to break the monotony and facilitate change."

Management

To support my psychological safety and get the best from me:

- Give me the new and risky assignments to keep me stimulated.
- Pair me with detail-oriented people to counteract my weakness.
- Avoid micromanagement—give me the big picture with a few critical rules.
- Do not put me in charge of risk management or detailed planning.
- Use me to explore the world and find risks to your business.

AUTONOMY

Ask people in a group setting, "Who likes to be told what to do?" Most of the time, no one raises their hand. Few of us like to be told what to do. Only occasionally, a hand will go up. Further exploration with that person usually reveals that what they are in fact craving is clarity. Their drive is to predict what is expected, how they will be measured, and how they will be rewarded. This falls into the Security domain. But once people have a sense of certainty, they usually don't like being told what to do. They want control over their environment.

Although our conscious response may appear to accept directions, at a nonconscious level our threat response can be triggered, and we resist. That resistance may be so strong that it sabotages our conscious efforts to listen and comply, particularly when directions are imposed upon us rather than chosen or invited. Our amygdala can perceive this intrusion as a threat and shut down our PFC, impacting our ability to process instructions.

We know from neuroscience research that people are more likely to succeed when they buy into an idea. When people reach their own insights and conclusions, solve their own problems, or come up with their own ideas, their brain gets a hit of the pleasure chemical dopamine, which helps facilitate action (Kounios, 2014). In this reward state, people are far more likely to own and implement solutions.

Modern coaching facilitates the coachees' thinking and allows them to come up with their own ideas. Only if they get stuck are people nudged with alternatives, and then they are given the opportunity to choose amongst those alternatives. Once again, the brain has a sense of choice and control.

Although this may only be a perception of control, it is the perception that really matters. To the brain, perception equals reality. The importance of perceived autonomy is demonstrated in patient-administered analgesia. The practice came about after studies showed that post-surgical patients who controlled their own pain medication administration used about half the morphine of patients who depended on the doctor or nurse to medicate them.

A body of research suggests that having little or no control leads to a state of learned helplessness, which can have a major impact on our health. It is commonly linked to depression, anxiety, and stress. The impact of autonomy on emotional and cognitive functioning is so profound that an animal model of learned helplessness is used to screen antidepressant drugs for humans (Stone, 2012). In the model, rats are assessed for how long they will tread water in a pool with no way out. Rats hate to get wet, so they will continue to tread water and search for an escape route until exhausted. After repeated trials in this pool, the rats realize that no matter how hard they try, they will never escape. Then something amazing happens: the rat gets placed in the pool and refuses to swim or search for an escape. It has given up the will to fight due to this learned sense of helplessness.

Studies have further shown that participants who experience a regular lack of autonomy or control usually produce an increased emotional response to stress. These people have also been shown to have an increased perception of pain, and lower longevity. In one study, it was demonstrated that people reporting a sense of helplessness had a five times greater chance of developing high blood pressure than those who didn't report feeling helpless (Stern, 2009).

While we all have some need for autonomy, it is reasonable to expect that the higher your need for autonomy, the greater the impact on you if you have no sense of control. Conversely, if you have a lower need for autonomy, then not having a sense of control might not impact you as profoundly.

Let's take the example of a person who has a high need for autonomy, and examine the process of setting goals for this person and their group. This person will want to be actively involved in setting the goals; imposing goals on him or her will be met with a high degree of (possibly nonconscious) resistance. In addition, he or she will likely be highly sensitive to being micromanaged in the way they go about achieving these goals, or in the way their progress is monitored.

What if that highly autonomous person is leading a group? This can manifest itself in a couple of ways. On the one hand, they may assume that everyone must be just like them, and thus need the same level of autonomy. We all tend to have a bias, known as the "false consensus bias," to think that people are just like us. Such a bias might result in the leader delegating too much and giving insufficient direction to those they lead.

On the other hand, the leader's need for control might be such that they are very directive and prescriptive to the people who work for them, to the point of micromanagement, despite the fact that they themselves do not like to be micromanaged.

AUTONOMY

Summary

- Autonomy is the feeling of control over one's environment (whether the control is real or not).
- A sensation of having choices within any given situation is rewarding to the brain.
- Lack of control, powerlessness, or helplessness, has a major impact on both our psychological and physical health.
- Autonomy reduces stress, pain perception, and hypertension.

Stop now and consider . . .

1. How important is it to you to have freedom over your life and choice in your decisions?
2. How do you react to being managed closely, or to having limitations put on you?

AUDREY
High Autonomy Need

Strengths

"I am self-confident, self-motivated, and express myself freely. I contribute independent, out-of-the-box thinking to the team and have incredible initiative. I am extremely low maintenance and don't require external motivation, direction, or management. You can count on me to instigate, run with, and deliver on initiatives with little direction. My independent perspectives can be the critical disruptor needed to kick-start creativity and innovation and provide valuable alternatives to the status quo."

Challenges

"My strong need for control, and my dislike for commitments, relationships, and situations that restrict my freedom, can lead me to avoid or resist situations that call for team interdependency or group socialization. I have been accused of being aloof and difficult to get to know, and some interpret my behavior as not being a team player. Because I am self-driven and need little instruction I tend to assume others are the same. This can be difficult for those who are looking for more direction and details.

"Under times of stress, or when highly triggered, I can become impatient with others as well as over-prescriptive and directive, or even take over a task to get it done. Being in control makes me feel safe, so I am nonconsciously driven to find ways to increase my sense of autonomy and control in times of stress."

Management

To support my psychological safety and get the best from me:

- Give me the big picture and the freedom to implement as I see fit.
- Avoid giving me advice unless asked.
- Where possible, allow me to work independently.
- Give me the feeling of having choices and don't force me into boxes.
- Avoid overcommunication and ultimatums.

ALEX

Low Autonomy Need

Strengths

"I am very open to receiving direction, and am a great follower and supporter. I am laid-back, and I like to follow others' lead while championing and supporting them in their visions and goals. I am a cooperative and easy-to-work-with team player, always happy to pitch in and do what is necessary. I am highly collaborative and very adaptable to any environment. I have an agreeable nature and an ability to get along with others, which promotes solidarity and harmony in the team."

Challenges

"I don't tend to be self-directed and can be easily swayed by the opinions of others, or influenced by group consensus. I sometimes have problems making decisions or taking a strong stance. I am not internally driven by a strong vision and don't tend to take control or lead others, which has the potential to limit my career progression. I can be overwhelmed, and get lost in situations that require me to be self-directed, to work alone, or to lead others."

"In times of stress, or when highly triggered, I seek strong external support and collaboration, and look for others to take the lead. I defer decisions to others and may deflect responsibility and accountability. Others being in control makes me feel safe, so I am nonconsciously driven to find ways to put others in the driver's seat in times of stress."

Management

To support my psychological safety and get the best from me:

- Avoid putting me in positions where I must make unpopular decisions.
- Don't push me to have opinions or make decisions when I don't want to.
- Provide me with clear direction and give me a lot of reinforcement that I am on the right track.
- Accept that I am willing to go along with decisions made by others.
- Don't expect me to have passionate opinions.

FAIRNESS

Fairness is a critical component in our perception of how we are treated and how others are treated. We all want to see and feel that we are treated fairly.

One of the roots of our need for fairness stems from our desire to receive an adequate allocation of the resources of our tribe. Without this drive for fairness, our ancestors might not have received the necessary share of food or shelter to survive and pass on their genes. Therefore, our brain learned to detect and respond strongly to fairness.

Studies of the brain have shown that when we perceive something as "unfair," an area of the brain called the insula is activated (Cheng, 2017). This region deals with the extremely important primary emotion of disgust, which compels us to be repulsed. As a species, we needed the disgust response because its activation by bitter food signaled that the food was probably poisonous. A strong aversion to poison made sense for our health and well-being.

Since our brain responds with this same intense emotion to unfairness, it would seem that having a strong aversion to being treated unfairly, or witnessing someone else being treated unjustly, is advantageous to us and our species. Interestingly, activation of the insula area interferes with the activation of the higher brain (PFC), once again affecting our brain's "braking system." So, perceiving unfairness can actually get in the way of managing our emotions.

On the other hand, when we see that something is fair, the reward system in our brain is activated and we get a release of the pleasure chemical dopamine, which makes us feel good and motivates us to seek out and value fairness (Tabibnia, 2007).

Let's take a look at a few examples across a spectrum of fairness. At one end we find two children arguing over who received a larger piece of cake, or who gets to sit in the front seat of the car. In the middle we see a group of people going on a hunger strike to fight against a real or perceived injustice. At the most extreme level, tribes or countries go to war to fight for principles of freedom and equality.

In these last two examples, people are willing to personally sacrifice, or even lay down their lives, to fight against unfairness or injustice. The scenarios highlight how intense the drive of this primal response can be.

Much research has examined the concept of fairness and how we perceive it. One study looked at fairness in the laboratory setting using something called the "Ultimatum Game" (Cheng, 2007). In this game, person A has a stake of money, say $50. They are told that they may offer person B a share of that $50. The catch is that unless person B agrees that person A has made a fair offer, neither party receives any money.

The outcomes suggest that person B rejects offers less than 20 percent of the initial stake; in this case, any amount below $10. In their mind, "person A has $50 and they're only giving me $10, so that's not really fair."

If our brains were purely rational, person B would accept any amount of money, because it's money that neither of them would have had otherwise. However, the brain is wired to detect unfairness and respond with disgust, shutting down rational thought.

Another piece of research on fairness looked at the opinions of convicted criminals within the U.S. judicial system. For any given offense, the imposed sentence can vary widely. The surprising finding was that how an offender felt about their sentence had much less to do with the length of the sentence than with how fairly he or she felt that the system had treated them.

In both of these examples, you can see that our perception of fairness has a lot to do with context, not just an absolute assessment of fairness.

FAIRNESS

Summary

- Fairness is our need for exchanges within our environment to be fair, both to us and to others.
- Fair exchanges are intrinsically rewarding to the brain. We all want to see and feel that we are treated fairly.
- Unfairness uses the same brain networks as disgust. It elicits the same primal emotion.
- When we perceive we are treated unfairly, our braking system weakens and we tend not to make rational decisions.

Stop now and consider . . .

1. How important is it for you to experience fairness and equality?
2. How do you react when you perceive there to be an injustice?

FRANK
High Fairness Need

Strengths

"I am a champion for justice and equality. I am a strong advocate for principles, standards, policies, and procedures that promote equity, fairness, and transparency, and hold us accountable. I am a nurturer and caretaker; I am empathetic to people's needs and bold in standing up for those who are unwilling or unable to do it themselves. I am highly collaborative and ensure everyone has the opportunity to contribute, has their voice heard, and is recognized for their contribution. I am a fair and dependable partner; my open and forthright nature ensures you always know where you stand."

Challenges

"My insistence on compliance to fair and inclusive practices by seeking group input and consensus can at times over-complicate the process and stagnate progress. Looking after everybody's interests and keeping them happy is important, but can derail focus and resources from productivity and results. I know some can get frustrated at my scrutiny for political correctness. I am very passionate and can at times be overzealous in my pursuit of justice.

"When I am stressed or highly triggered I can be inclined to hold a grudge or even sacrifice my personal interests to take revenge or get retribution for an injustice. Environments of justice and equality make me feel safe, so I am nonconsciously driven to find ways to seek and administer justice in times of stress."

Management

To support my psychological safety and get the best from me:

- Create and utilize policies that are applied fairly to everyone—avoid favoritism.
- Allow me to contribute and have my voice heard.
- Ensure transparency, especially in decision-making processes.
- Avoid faint praise or unearned rewards.
- Ensure equity in exchanges and expectations.

FAY

Low Fairness Need

Strengths

"I am great at execution and implementation; I don't let people and dogma restrain me. I am prepared to do the necessary dirty work to get results. I am not derailed by drama or constrained by emotional issues during deliberations. I am able to compartmentalize and cut through the noise when negotiating or making decisions. I am direct and honest in my communications and know how to identify and take full advantage of opportunities that present themselves."

Challenges

"Some do not appreciate my practical approach to progress. I understand that my opinions, decisions, and methods are not always popular and can sometimes be perceived as hard-nosed or cold. My opportunistic nature can come off as leveraging others' disadvantage or using unconventional means to get ahead. But at the end of the day . . . I get results.

"In times of stress my drive for results is heightened. I will focus on tangible results and use money, innovation, and progress as motivators to enlist the support of others. Because achieving results makes me feel safe, I am nonconsciously driven to be goal focused in times of stress, and will find ways to work around processes or constraints that hold me back."

Management
To support my psychological safety and get the best from me:
- Do not place political correctness over results.
- Focus on outcomes rather than processes or methods.
- Avoid discussions about social issues.
- Do not use fairness as a motivator but focus on alternative drivers to motivate action.

ESTEEM

The reward areas of our brain are activated when we regard ourselves highly and when we think others regard us highly. Interestingly, the same region of the brain that responds to the thrill of winning money also fires in response to a compliment.

Let's revisit the experiment conducted by UCLA researchers. The brain activity of subjects was measured as they played a game of cyber ball with what they were told were two strangers. Initially, the subject was playing a game of virtual "catch" with two other participants and everyone was included. At a certain point the subject was excluded from the game. In reality, no other people were playing. The "strangers" were simply a computer program. This went on for a few minutes, and the subject invariably became frustrated. Brain imaging confirmed that the pain areas of the brain were activated.

Social rejection, by way of public insult or a challenge to our esteem, has the same impact on the brain as a punch to the face. Rejection activates our pain networks.

To test this idea, the researchers proposed that drugs which relieve physical pain should also help with social pain, and that's exactly what they found. By giving people who were experiencing social pain a dose of acetaminophen, they were able to demonstrate a reduction in the behavioral and brain responses associated with pain (DeWall, 2014).

What's more, research suggests that the impact of social pain seems to be longer lasting and more profound than that of physical pain.

In this section, we'll explore three different parts of this domain:

- How we see ourselves, that is, our self-esteem
- How we compare ourselves to others
- How we think others see us

HOW WE SEE OURSELVES

Our self-esteem is fundamental for both our health and our survival. In studies of gorillas, alpha males who were taken out of the pack and put into a new group where they were made subservient to the rest of the pack, developed ulcers and died sooner. Human research also points to the importance of esteem.

Several studies have suggested that children who identified as having low esteem are, as adults, much more easily stressed and more likely to suffer from anxiety. In addition, recent research has demonstrated that such children have a more reactive amygdala in response to fearful situations. As the emotional center of our brain drives the threat response, children with lower self-esteem have a more difficult time managing emotions and are susceptible to a strong negativity bias (Muscatell, 2012).

Our self-evaluations, which determine our self-esteem, are based on the images we hold of ourselves. They can be positive or negative, and they impact how we feel about ourselves. When we feel good about ourselves, we become less sensitive to stress, are healthier, and tend to live longer.

We also hold images of what we could become, our "possible selves." These range from a highly positive outlook of the future on the one hand to a darkly negative view on the other, and each of these views drives our sense of self. This in turn drives our mindset, or ability to see ourselves succeeding or failing in future endeavors, and can be a determining factor as to whether or not we achieve our goals.

A good example of this is dieting. People want to lose weight, so they set goals for eating healthier and exercising more. However, when they don't see immediate results, their self-esteem is challenged and they may develop a negative mindset, which can lead to a downward emotional spiral.

HOW WE COMPARE OURSELVES WITH OTHERS

We compare ourselves with others on many levels. Am I fatter or thinner, richer or poorer, do I have a bigger house or smaller house? These comparisons usually happen on a nonconscious level, and the more we feel that we come up short in the comparison, the less confident we feel about ourselves.

HOW WE THINK OTHERS SEE US

Another factor influencing our esteem is how we think others see us. Critical to this esteem driver is the perception of disapproval. Research has shown that disapproval from others activates the amygdala even more than fear (Burkland, 2007). So, if your parents or trusted mentors expressed disappointment in you, it likely had more of an impact than when they were angry at you.

This is similar in the workplace. If you have ever held the position of leader or teammate and you indicated either directly or through body language that you were disappointed in another person (particularly in a public setting), then you were having more impact on their brain than if you had been angry or physically threatening! In such a situation, with their behavior now being primarily driven by their lower brain, this person will be less creative, less focused, and less productive.

Conversely, the reward areas of the brain are activated when we receive compliments or are told that we have a good reputation (Phan, 2012). We pay attention to what others think of us and actually build maps about what we think other people think of us. Of course, our brain likes consistency so these maps of how others see us need to align with how we feel about ourselves. If this isn't the case (e.g. someone sees us in a negative light when we feel that we are a good person), then it influences our relationship with that person and how we engage, respond, and react to him or her.

ESTEEM

Summary

- Esteem covers our view of ourselves and how we compare to others, and how we think others view us.
- Our reward areas are activated when we regard ourselves highly and when we think others regard us highly.
- Threats to our esteem can increase our fear and negativity bias response.

Stop now and consider . . .

1. How important is it for you to be held in high regard?
2. How do you react when your self-esteem or status is being challenged?

ERIC
High Esteem Need

Strengths

"I am an energetic, ambitious, and fun influence on the team. I am a tremendous networker—I mix in the 'right' circles and seek out those with power and influence. I am driven by success and enjoy the challenge of lofty targets. My professional image and list of accomplishments reflects confidence and credibility. I do well in social settings, and am often the life of the party. I am charismatic and engaging and a skilled storyteller, able to sell myself and my ideas. I keep spirits high and am able to put on a happy face even in the face of adversity."

Challenges

"It is very important to me to be regarded highly by others. At times this can result in overextending myself or 'performing' to impress. I know that some interpret my competitive spirit as a game of one-upmanship and a need to be better than others. Being heavily influenced by the opinions and approval of others, I will often refrain from expressing my opinions or ideas in fear that they will be unpopular or rejected.

"Under stress or when highly triggered, I can become very defensive in my justification of myself or my actions. High esteem makes me feel safe, so I am nonconsciously driven to find ways to justify my worth and increase my status in times of stress."

Management

To support my psychological safety and get the best from me:

- Offer praise and recognition (preferably in public).
- Deliver criticism and feedback for improvement delicately.
- Avoid one-upmanship or appearing to compete directly with me.
- Avoid putting me in situations where I need to make unpopular decisions or where I will be cast in a negative light.
- Motivate me by offering status gains.

ESTA

Low Esteem Need

Strengths

"I am self-confident and independent-minded, not easily shaken or swayed by trends or the opinion of others. I am self-motivated and confident in my abilities; I follow my own internal compass and am not easily corrupted by social pressure. I am a team player who enjoys sharing credit for collaborative wins and I encourage others by promoting, acknowledging, and celebrating their successes."

Challenges

"I don't tend to conform or perform to meet other's expectations, and tend to play down my achievements. Some interpret my personal and professional contentment as showing a lack of ambition as I don't play the 'success game.' Being unmotivated by and unimpressed by status symbols, comparison measures, and images that are perceived as markers of success can work against me in networking and sales settings where the outcome is determined by image and self-promotion. My discomfort with acknowledgement can also rob others of the joy of giving me praise and recognition.

"In times of stress or when pressured to conform or compete I will deflect attention and look to close down or exit the forum. I will strongly defend my independence of thought and will stay steadfast to my personal goals and convictions. Authenticity and modesty make me feel safe, so I am nonconsciously driven to find ways to stay true to myself and avoid the limelight in times of stress."

Management

To support my psychological safety and get the best from me:
- Avoid comparing me to others.
- Avoid using peer pressure as a tool of change.
- Recognize me in private and avoid putting me in the spotlight.
- Expect status rewards to be less effective and use other triggers to motivate action.
- Do not expect me to play the game of one-upmanship.

TRUST

Our brain empathizes most with those who are similar to us and likable, and sees strangers as a threat. From a survival perspective, this makes absolute sense. Let's revisit the tribal setting and consider a stranger arriving unannounced in our territory. It's a safe bet that they did not come for pleasant reasons but were far more likely to present a threat to our lives and be after our resources.

So our brain, in its quest to maintain our safety by monitoring for danger and quickly reacting to threats, assumes by default that something or someone could be dangerous unless proven otherwise.

What are the implications? Well, think about that lower brain for a second. It will immediately categorize people into one of two groups—friend or foe. This is commonly referred to as the "in-group" versus the "out-group." It turns out that our brain's default response is to treat all strangers as belonging to the "out-group." Since this all happens below the level of consciousness it is difficult to be aware of, let alone manage, this categorization. The result is an instinctive bias against those perceived as outside our realm of "safety" (Mobbs, 2009).

Finding commonality with the outsider is one of the most effective techniques for managing this in-group vs. out-group dilemma. When we identify commonalities, we actually start to think about the outsider with the part of our brain used to reflect upon ourselves, enabling us to be more trusting. In essence, we switch the area of the brain dealing with the newcomer and move the person to that part of the brain that is recruited for in-group processing (Ames, 2008).

The good news is that creating an in-group can happen fairly quickly. To illustrate this point, in some of our workshops we ask the question "Who owns a dog?" Then we start a discussion about dogs and dog ownership. Most dog owners are passionate, not only about dogs, but about the particular breed they own.

Within minutes there is a lively discussion going on between the dog owners. We have created an in-group. Trust has significantly increased between the members of this group. But what has happened to the people who are not dog owners? They often report feeling left out of the discussion and experiencing a sense of rejection. This all takes place in two or three minutes.

The power of the in-group vs. out-group struggle is illustrated in a striking experiment conducted to examine empathy (Xu, 2009). In the study, researchers examined Chinese and Caucasian subjects who had their brain patterns recorded while they watched a video of someone piercing their cheek.

In one version, the participant witnessed someone from their own race experience the pain (i.e. a Caucasian subject watching a Caucasian victim, or a Chinese subject watching a Chinese victim). In another version, the participant viewed the subject of the opposite race experience the same activity (Caucasian subject watching a Chinese victim, or Chinese subject watching a Caucasian victim). The researchers focused on a specific area of the brain called the Anterior Cingulate Cortex (ACC), which we think deals with the emotional component of empathy.

Results of the study indicated that when subjects watched someone from their own race experience discomfort, their "empathy" brain network activated, yet this was not the case for participants witnessing someone from another race undergo the same procedure. This was one of the first studies to verify neural evidence of an in-group vs. out-group bias.

Fortunately, as humans we have the unique ability to manage this "us vs. them" brain response through a cognitive or reasoning component managed by our higher brain (PFC) that we can call on to override the automatic, nonconscious emotional reaction of our lower brain.

To illustrate how this in-group vs. out-group works without any regulation from the PFC, think about your dog's response to you (his in-group) versus to a stranger (his out-group). He sees you walk into the house and responds by wagging his tail and wanting to play. If a stranger walks in the house, the dog barks, growls, and maybe even tries to attack.

We humans use logic and knowledge from past experiences to override our nonconscious in-group vs. out-group responses. This was reflected in the study outlined above where, despite the fact that the brain's empathy response was only active for victims of the same race (i.e. their in-group), all subjects verbally reported experiencing empathy for every one of the victims, regardless of their race.

This is good news, as it sets us apart from the rest of the animal kingdom. We are not slaves to our primal nature. If I encountered you as a stranger in an elevator, despite a nonconscious desire to relegate you to my out-group, I am able to rise above my primal instinct to be fearful and defensive, and manage to avoid backing into the corner, barking, and trying to exert my dominance over you.

Remember, however, that this ability to override our amygdala's emotional response and engage the cognitive reasoning of our PFC is limited, and exposure to too much stress can diminish our control. When this happens, we are more susceptible to the negativity bias and the in-group vs. out-group reaction.

TRUST

Summary

- We are social animals who thrive in tribes. Our brains empathize most with those who are similar to us and likable: our in-group.
- The brain treats strangers as a threat, categorizing them as a "foe," and processes them as part of our out-group.
- We are able to override this nonconscious out-group bias towards strangers by engaging our PFC and finding commonalities with them.
- Stress can severely decrease our ability to override this bias.

Stop now and consider . . .

1. How important is it for you to feel like you belong and that people in your group are loyal?
2. How do you react when you feel rejected or when you believe people have betrayed your trust?

TRACY

High Trust Need

Strengths

"I am the social glue of the team. I bring people together and create strong group cohesion, culture, and team uniformity. I am excellent at recognizing a good 'cultural fit' in recruitment processes. I am collaborative and inclusive and tend to be the network node of the group. I build strong social connections and relationships, and am fiercely loyal to, and protective of, the team."

Challenges

"I know that my highly collaborative nature and focus on social considerations has the potential to distract people's focus and impact productivity. Sometimes my fierce loyalty, along with my sensitivity to rejection, can make me prioritize others' needs over my self-interests. I champion the group's alignment to established norms and a defined culture, but that can make the team susceptible to groupthink and a fixed mindset, and limit our openness to diversity of people and ideas. It also has the potential to impact the team's agility and resilience, as it is ill-prepared for change and evolution.

"Under times of stress or when highly triggered by a trust threat, I tend to view situations through an 'us vs. them' lens, and relegate people to either the in-group, those to be included, or the out-group, those to be excluded. A sense of trust and belonging makes me feel safe, so I am nonconsciously driven to find ways to protect my place in the group. I have a heightened sensitivity to loyalty during times of stress."

Management

To support my psychological safety and get the best from me:

- Motivate me with wording that emphasizes the team, for example, use "we" instead of "I."
- Be open and willing to share with me on a personal level to establish commonality.
- Show loyalty and avoid displays or actions that could suggest disloyalty.
- In collaborative situations, leverage my skills to help bring people together.
- Be especially empathetic with me.

TRENT
Low Trust Need

Strengths

"I am open-minded, comfortable networking in diverse environments, and like to explore connections with people from nonstandard places and outside of traditional norms. I foster multi-dimensional and diverse relationships that challenge new and independent thinking. I don't tend to fall victim to or employ in-group/out-group manipulation strategies that can cause division and offense. I can be left to my own devices and can work quietly without social distraction."

Challenges

"Because I tend to resist environments where in-groups gather, some interpret my behavior as being non-collaborative and lacking team spirit. I know some perceive my behavior as antisocial and even introverted. My unwillingness to comply with group rituals, traditions, and norms is unsettling for some, leading them to speculate about my intentions and question my loyalty.

"In times of stress I will avoid situations that pressure me to conform to groupthink or group behaviors. I will react strongly to being boxed in and labeled, and will seek refuge in solitary activities or by moving to a different social circle. Being independent and free from herd mentality makes me feel safe, so I am nonconsciously driven to find ways to detach myself from restrictive group expectations and behaviors during times of stress."

Management

To support my psychological safety and get the best from me:
- Don't force me to be in, or join, groups.
- Respect my non-compliance to ritual, traditions, and norms.
- Allow me to work alone rather than in groups.
- Avoid using the threat of exclusion or rejection as a tool of change.
- Expect "inclusion" or "loyalty" rewards to be less effective, and use other triggers to motivate action.

YOU

While the five previous sections covered the domains that apply to all of us collectively, the "Y" domain is highly individualistic and therefore much more complex. Think of this domain as encompassing the factors that help explain what drives your individual needs on a day-to-day, or moment-to-moment, basis as you navigate your experiences, desires, and attitudes. Some of these factors may include your personality profile, your past experiences, your genetic influences, your social influences, your biases, your beliefs, your goals, your mood, and your stress levels, just to name a few.

Understanding your personal influences may offer valuable insights into your behavior and motivations. This self-reflection can provide keys to improving and building your effectiveness and your relationships.

In order to illustrate the importance of this domain, let's talk about Ron, a 43-year-old executive who constantly micromanages his team.

When Ron was a young child, he often played a favorite game with his father. This involved climbing onto a stool, shouting, "Daddy, daddy, catch me!" and then jumping into his father's arms. One day, however, his father stepped back and allowed Ron to fall. As Ron stood up, feeling rejected, hurt, and disappointed, his father said to him, "Let that be a lesson to you. Never. Trust. Anyone!"

Ron learned his father's lesson well, and as an adult he practices it on his team every day. He lacks close relationships with the team members and often questions their commitment, their motivations, and their intentions. He does not trust them to deliver on expectations and demands constant tracking and reassurance that they are keeping to deadlines.

YOU

Summary

- Individual variables make you *you*, and account for your moment-to-moment moods and motivations.
- Your past experiences and genetic influences help determine your responses to the other five SAFETY domains.
- Aspects that can impact this domain are your personality; your biases, patterns, habits and triggers; your past experiences; your future plans; your current situation; and your current outlook.
- The impact of this domain can be so strong that it can outweigh any or all of the other five.

S.A.F.E.T.Y.™ Model Summary

The S.A.F.E.T.Y.™ model helps us understand what we need in order to feel psychologically safe. When we experience a threat to the SAFETY domains, we are triggered into a stress response where our PFC goes offline and we are at the mercy of the automated emotional brain. So if our goal is to stay in the driver's seat of our thinking and behavior, it is important that we become conscious protectors of psychological safety and seek to minimize the triggers that threaten it.

The high and low character profile examples given earlier were intentionally exaggerated in order to highlight their traits. You are unlikely to find living versions this extreme. In truth we are all motivated by each SAFETY domain to some degree, but we differ in the way our brains respond to them. Our unique collection of experiences has mapped our brain with particular sensitivities that determine the importance we place on each domain.

Someone who has experienced positive outcomes from change in their life may require a much more severe situation before their Autonomy or Security is threatened than someone who has had a series of negative experiences with life changes. This is not to say that the individual with positive experiences craves ambiguity, rather that their brain has mapped their experiences in such a way that they may see day-to-day changes as less threatening. Because of this it is important to be aware of our own, and others', thresholds (the "Y" in action).

You may be able to recognize yourself or others in some of these domains, and at this point you might like to reflect on each of the characters presented and consider how they resonate with you. How would you prioritize the order of the first five (SAFET) SAFETY domains for you, with one being the highest and five being the lowest?

If you are interested in knowing your SAFETY profile and its impacts, you can find more information about the SAFETY online self-assessment on pages 156–159.

S.A.F.E.T.Y.™ FOCUS LEVELS

So where to from here?

Now that you understand the components of psychological safety, we want to suggest a concentric approach to increasing your awareness and skills to best manage and facilitate it. For SAFETY to thrive, it needs to have focus at the following four levels, working from the inside out:

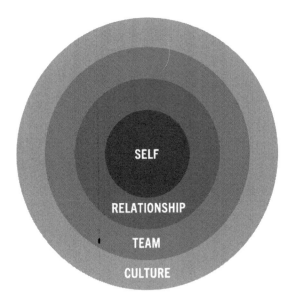

Self

At the center of everything is the understanding of self. You can dispel the mystery and control of the nonconscious brain by becoming conscious of your drivers and triggers. Then, rather than being blindly led by an invisible leash, you can assume control and responsibility and be accountable for directing and guiding your internal and external dialogue and behaviors.

Psychologically Safe Individuals:
- Take responsibility for their SAFETY drivers and their impact
- Protect and express their SAFETY needs
- Catch and manage their SAFETY triggers
- Understand how their SAFETY biases influence their perspective
- Appreciate the SAFETY perspectives of others

Relationship

Once you have a handle on yourself and understand how your drivers color your world and your perspective, you can begin to look at how that influences your interactions and relationships with others.

Individuals in Psychologically Safe Relationships:
- Protect and nurture each other's SAFETY needs
- Are sensitive to each other's SAFETY drivers and triggers
- Are empathetic to each other's SAFETY perspective
- Are able to take a SAFETY approach to conflicts

Team

Once you have your interpersonal SAFETY skills honed, you can apply SAFETY to the team context. Teams are a melting pot of all three levels, an eclectic collection of selves who are navigating their relationships in order to achieve team success. Bringing all three levels into the psychological safety commitment is important. With everyone on the same page, the team can harness individual momentum and build structures and support that will foster a psychologically safe environment.

Members of Psychologically Safe Teams:
- Value psychological safety and are accountable to it
- Protect and nurture the SAFETY of self, relationships, and team
- Harness the strength of the SAFETY diversity of its members
- Promote transparency and openness
- Are not afraid to expose vulnerability or admit mistakes
- Feel safe to take risks or offer opinions

Culture

Real change happens where psychological safety is adopted and normalized at a systemic level. Culture sets the tone, language, and expectations across a population; it informs process and practice; and holds people accountable to particular standards.

When psychological safety is identified and embraced as a cultural priority there is a drive from the top ensuring that psychological safety is supported and woven into the fabric of the system at all levels. In this best-case scenario, buy-in and accountability are driven both from the bottom up (self) and the top down (culture).

Psychologically Safe Cultures:
- Value and promote psychological safety as a cultural standard
- Speak the language of SAFETY
- Foster psychological safety through policy and process
- Monitor psychological safety as a health performance indicator at all levels

Although we strive for the ideal and one day hope for it to be a reality, we don't need to wait for all four levels to be aligned before we start looking after our own and each other's psychological safety.

With this approach in mind, let's continue the self-awareness path and explore what you can do to increase your SAFETY capacity and how that links into relationship awareness.

SELF & RELATIONSHIP SAFETY

Know Your Biases

Hopefully by now you are able to identify with some of the characters presented, and you are becoming aware of the SAFETY drivers that are important to you at the level of "Self." The next step is understanding how your drivers color your world and your perspectives. This is closely interwoven with the level of "Relationships." Your SAFETY paradigms have important implications for your interactions and relationships with others.

We are all tainted by SAFETY biases. They are the paradigm by which we perceive and judge our world and the people around us. Because of the confirmation bias, your brain is always scanning the environment for evidence to support your existing paradigms. Your brain seeks to confirm and reinforce what you hold to be true, and ignores or rejects evidence to the contrary.

With these SAFETY biases in play you have a natural tendency to speculate about and interpret other people's behaviors and attitudes, their motivation or intent, in accordance with your biases. You create narratives that map their behavior to the checklist of your existing paradigm, and evaluate if this experience is consistent with, or disconnected from, previous experiences.

This serves to confirm your assumptions about the world and increases your certainty, which makes you feel safe.

The problem with this is that your judgments can derail or even deceive you, and you can fall into the trap of interpreting benign or neutral behaviors as threats. When others don't act or think the way you do, or the way you think they should, you experience a cognitive disconnect. Your brain likes to be right. It operates with this assumption as its default, so it resolves any cognitive disconnect by determining that the behaviors or thought processes of others are "wrong."

Your "old" emotional brain takes the path of least resistance, preferring to reject the other person and their behavior, beliefs, or opinions, rather than do the hard work of engaging your rational higher brain to challenge your assumptions and remap this new information into your paradigm. This often leads to a stalemate where both parties hold fast to their own paradigm, dig in their heels, and defend their positions. The result is a win/lose battle, where one or both parties walk away unheard and wounded.

Remember, these filters and checklists are highly individualized. There is no overarching agreement on what is "good" or "bad." You are playing and judging by your own rule book, one that has been constructed over time by your "old brain." You evaluate and judge situations and others' actions against these unwritten rules, rules that they don't know, did not agree to, and didn't sign up for.

You may mistakenly attribute a sinister motivation to some behaviors and choose to interpret them from the perspective of your triggered domain. These perceptions and assumptions are the perfect environment for breeding offense and disconnection, and can contribute to the construction of walls and deterioration of relationships.

Have you ever gone down this path and cast your judgments, only to find out, after getting more background or information about the other person's perspective, that your assumptions about them and their behavior were wrong?

Let's revisit our SAFETY characters and look at a few examples of how we may work from different paradigms and essentially speak different safety languages that set us up for offense and disconnect.

SCENARIO 1: Tracy & Audrey
High Trust Need vs. High Autonomy Need

Tracy's perspective: "As a connector and relationship builder, I have made a lot of effort to embrace Audrey, who is new to the team. I am particularly sensitive to people feeling alienated, and look for ways to give them a sense of belonging. Although Audrey is cordial and polite, she has not accepted any of my invitations to various team socials or events since she arrived.

"I am so offended that she has not engaged or responded to my hospitality and outreach. It isn't normal. I am not sure I trust her; I am not sure she is a good fit here. We have certain ways of doing things, and she doesn't seem like a team player. I think she is deliberately shutting me out to let me know she doesn't like me. That's fine, two can play that game!"

Audrey's perspective: "I am really excited by this new opportunity and my new job, but I am not necessarily here for the social interaction. Tracy doesn't seem to have any appreciation for others' personal boundaries. I just want to settle in and find my feet. She seems very needy and keeps trying to get me involved. I am finding her a bit suffocating. She doesn't seem to be getting the hint when I don't engage or respond to invitations.

"Can't she see I am not interested? I'll engage when and how I want to. The last thing I need to deal with right now is a high-maintenance person putting pressure on me with their neediness and expectations. I think this is her laying the ground rules and setting the expectations for what it means to be a team player."

SCENARIO 2: Eric & Frank
High Esteem Need vs. High Fairness Need

Eric's perspective: "Had an amazing meeting with management today. What a great opportunity to share about the large account I landed this week! I think I really impressed them. It's a great addition to the company portfolio. This definitely reinforces my value and contribution to the company. Hopefully it will result in a promotion or a bonus! Of course, Frank is ticked off with me again. He's never a supporter. He always seems to want to cut me down. He's probably jealous."

Frank's perspective: "How dare Eric take full credit for winning that account when it was totally a team effort! He deliberately short-changed all those who contributed, purely for his own gain. I think I need to meet with management to set the record straight. It would be completely unfair if Eric were to solely benefit from everyone else's hard work, especially when many of us did more than he did to get it over the line. We all need to share the glory for this one. I am not going to let him get away with this."

SCENARIO 3: Sam & Seth
High Security Need vs. Low Security Need

Sam's perspective: "We have this road show coming up and there are so many factors to consider. I have prepared a detailed itinerary, done all the planning and scheduling, and have investigated what we need for each country and any risks associated with the travel.

"This is supposed to be a collaborative effort between Seth and me, yet I seem to be doing all the work. My requests for input and support largely go unanswered, and he seems completely unwilling to engage. It is like he is being deliberately evasive and uncooperative. That doesn't give me a lot of confidence in his reliability or follow-through on commitments."

Seth's perspective: "I am very excited about this road show. Sam is great at having all the bases covered and the details dealt with, but he can be a bit over the top. I am not as caught up in the intricacies as he is. If we have the broad strokes covered, we can handle the details when we get there.

"Most of the time, the contingencies he plans for never happen, so it seems like a waste of time to me. That said, I know he feels better dotting all the i's and crossing all the t's so I just leave him to it. I'm happy to go along with the plan, but I begrudge his expectation that I waste my time on the minutia."

See how our perspectives on the same situation can be like ships passing in the night? In none of these scenarios did anyone take time to consider the other person's perspective. They evaluated the situation, established motivations, and drew their conclusions based on only one set of data points—their own SAFETY rules!

This is understandable, as your SAFETY paradigms are firmly embedded. You have spent your entire lifetime filtering your experiences through them. They are your truth and your reality. It isn't easy to see life through an unfamiliar filter.

Understanding the insecurities and fears that motivate others can be tricky, particularly those who are driven by different SAFETY domains like the High Trust Need (Tracy) vs. High Autonomy Need (Audrey) exchange above, or who have an opposite sensitivity to you, like the High Security Need (Sam) vs. Low Security Need (Seth) exchange above.

In either case, the other person's way of thinking— their worldview, their filters and paradigms—are foreign to you and may even drive you crazy. Because the brain interprets the unknown and unfamiliar as "dangerous" and "unsafe," when you are triggered it's easy to villainize the "other" and their behavior to justify the hurt and offense caused by the violation to your SAFETY.

However, there are no right and wrong, or good and bad, SAFETY profiles. They all have a role, and they are all doing their job of protecting us and keeping us safe from those things that have threatened us in the past.

Appreciating this, it can serve you well to assume that others are genuinely motivated to be good people, to do their best, and not to deliberately hurt or offend you. In addition, if you can genuinely appreciate your differences and acknowledge that "it's not them, it's their brain," it is easier to take a compassionate and generous approach to others. In this way you can develop a sensitivity for psychological safety and minimize the harmful impact of being triggered and triggering others.

The more you can expose yourself to how others perceive the world, through sharing and perspective-taking, the more you can develop your sensitivity to triggers and begin to consider the SAFETY factors in your daily life.

KNOW YOUR BIASES

- Develop your self-awareness by identifying your SAFETY drivers and triggers, and reflecting on their potential impact on you and on others.
- Catch your biases and their influence on your perspective.
- Practice perspective-taking to challenge your paradigm and broaden your awareness of others.

Manage Your Triggers with T.R.A.I.N.™

So how do we stay in the driver's seat when we get triggered? How do we avoid jumping to conclusions that lead us down the slippery slope to offense?

Let us introduce you to T.R.A.I.N.™, a brain-based approach to managing your triggers and building psychologically safe relationships.

T.R.A.I.N.™ stands for:
- Trigger
- Reflect
- Appraise
- Include
- Neutralize

TRIGGER

Triggers occur when there is a violation to your SAFETY, and your "old brain" feels unsafe. First, you need to dampen that emotional response and get back in the driver's seat. You can achieve this most effectively by acknowledging the trigger and labeling your emotion.

It takes practice not to ride the wave of emotion that leads to offense, and learning to master that logical, rational, higher brain can be a bumpy road. To understand the brain science behind emotional regulation, let's look at a couple of experiments that investigated the impact of emotional suppression.

In the first experiment, researchers showed subjects an arousing video clip (a close-up of an arm amputation surgery). One group was asked to suppress their emotion expression behavior (their facial expressions) as much as possible during the clip, whereas the second group was free to express their emotions any way they wished. Researchers then gave the subjects a memory test for specific details of the clip, to see if there was a difference between the recall in the two groups. In a second study, subjects were shown a clip of a couple arguing. Researchers tasked a third group with distracting themselves (by thinking about something else) while watching the video instead of suppressing their emotions.

The group that was told to suppress their emotions was poorer at recalling details than the expressive group. The more intense the emotions evoked by the video (i.e. the more suppression needed), the poorer the memory recall became (Goldin, 2008). The same findings applied for both the surgery clip and the clip of people arguing. The researchers found that subjects who distracted themselves also experienced a decrease in recall, but not as much as the group who actively suppressed their emotional response. The researchers postulated that trying not to show emotion takes mental energy, which pulls resources away from cognitive processes.

In addition, suppressing your emotions puts you at risk of impacting your health and the health of those around you. Research has shown that by suppressing your negative emotions, your stress response is heightened, as is the stress response of those around you (Koenigsberg, 2010).

So what is the better way to manage your emotions?

Brain science has revealed that by simply labeling or naming the emotion you are feeling, you can dampen the amygdala response (Lieberman, 2007). When you need to analyze and recognize an emotion by naming it, you're forcing yourself to move into that analytical, higher brain (PFC) for a split second, which means you at least temporarily move out of the "old," emotional reactive brain. This split second can be enough to interrupt the trigger and allow you to reappraise or dampen its impact so that you don't react.

REFLECT

This is where you can enlist the help of your PFC to override the automated shortcuts that quickly measure and JUDGE. You can put the brakes on your "old brain" and engage your logical brain to acknowledge your paradigm and the non-conscious drivers that are influencing your perspective.

To do this requires meta-cognition, the act of thinking about your thinking. Research has found that engaging in this type of reflection activates a network in the brain called the "default mode network." This default mode can help you generate insights and see different perspectives (Moran, 2013). Rather than being a passive victim of that "old brain" narrative, you become an active observer of it. Taking an impartial spectator's seat, you can reflect on the merit of the accusations and assumptions rising out of that triggered brain from a neutral position.

APPRAISE

From this neutral vantage point you now have the opportunity to rewrite the story and choose how you interpret it.

This is the skill of appraisal and the art of perspective-taking. It is consciously putting aside the negative interpretation that caused your trigger response, and seeking other neutral or positive interpretations that may challenge your assumptions, beliefs, and attitudes.

This route is more resource intensive and will be met with resistance from your "old brain," which will highlight and justify your outrage by recalling memories and evoking emotions that are designed to keep you away from danger. But hold fast and push through. The appraisal process has positive health and relationship benefits.

Appraisal is a way of taking an alternative approach to a situation, one which diffuses the emotional distress that may be present. Let's say I'm standing in a long, slow-moving line at the supermarket checkout counter, where it's apparent that the only reason for the delay is a talkative checkout clerk. She's sharing personal stories with every customer. Meanwhile, I'm late for a dinner party and the line isn't moving.

I start to feel my frustration build in my gut and, having a high need for autonomy and control, it's too much to bear. I can suppress these feelings, but I know from the research that this just makes things worse . . . Maybe others in line will pick up on my anger and that will exacerbate their frustration . . .

HOWEVER, I could appraise this situation. Maybe this woman is recently divorced and has no one at home to talk to . . . She's lonely and this is her only opportunity to have human interaction all day. We all know the importance of having regular human contact, so this woman is simply trying to maintain her sanity during the day by connecting with others . . .

Now I've diffused the situation into one where I can appreciate possible reasons why this clerk is behaving the way she is, and the threat response is diminished.

Research has found that appraising situations in this manner can dampen the response in the amygdala and decrease the feelings of disgust associated with emotional overdrive and suppression (Martin, 2016). Appraisal in this manner helps you respect differences and acknowledge the needs of others by taking the time to view things from their SAFETY perspective. It helps disarm your trigger and diffuse the offense.

INCLUDE

Neuroscience research has shown that we use distinct areas of our brain when we think about ourselves versus when we think about others, that in-group vs. out-group process again. However, research has also shown that if you increase your exposure to others who are different from you, it will cause your brain to "relax" its negativity bias towards possible out-group members (Ames, 2008).

It has also been demonstrated that simply taking a first-person perspective of someone else's mindset (ideally in a written form), you start to use the part of your brain reserved to ponder yourself for thinking about the other person. The result is a higher likelihood of bringing people toward your in-group, and creating psychological safety.

One way to enhance your brain's ability to create a bias towards bringing people into your 'In' group is to simply increase your exposure to diverse groups and cultures. Remember that research by Xu and colleagues mentioned earlier, which suggested that our brains have an empathy bias against others who are different from us? Well, it turns out that follow-up research with subjects who had significant exposure to those different races didn't display this empathy bias in their brain! So by embracing diversity your brain actually makes it easier for you to see the world from another's perspective, thus building psychological safety (Cao, 2015).

Making psychological safety a priority moves you into neutral territory and allows you to realign to the common goal, thus facilitating the in-group mentality.

Acknowledging that "it's not them, it's their brain" can help depersonalize inflammatory situations and defuse your emotional response. Appreciating that a manifested trigger is a response to insecurities and fears can help you gain insight into others when confronted with triggering situations. Ask yourself, "What do those traits and behaviors tell me about the insecurities or fears that this person is protecting? What SAFETY domain is being threatened?"

This can be especially helpful when particular traits or behaviors are grating or repellent to you. They are not wrong, they are just different. Being generous in your approach and compassionate to their SAFETY needs helps humanize the situation.

NEUTRALIZE

Having calmed down your amygdala by acknowledging and labeling the trigger, reflecting on your biased perspective, reappraising your interpretation, and realigning to the common goal, you are ready to engage on neutral territory. Now considering the amazing plasticity of the brain, it should come as no surprise that by implementing some of these strategies you are actually "teaching" your brain to change. Appraisal is a good example. We know that reframing a situation in this manner can help dampen our negativity bias in the moment. However, in our everyday lives it would be beneficial for the effects of regulation to endure over time. Research has shown that regularly engaging in reappraisal can have long-lasting effects on emotional reactions to stimuli (Denny, 2015). The amygdala response becomes automatically dampened, without having to exert much effort. In essence, you have embedded this emotional regulation within the neural networks and can now engage others in a more neutral, psychologically-safe manner.

Acknowledge that the truth and the solution are likely somewhere between both perspectives. You can diffuse toxic situations and relationships through communication and a willingness to be vulnerable and transparent with one another about what drives you and triggers you. It is possible to respect and empathize with where the other is coming from.

Of course this conversation is better facilitated when both parties are committed to psychological safety, are versed in SAFETY, understand their drivers, and speak the language of SAFETY. By establishing a common language in this manner, we are able to appease the threat-based brain by seeing this person as part of our in-group, thus being better able to relate to his or her perspective.

Overcoming conflict and finding productive ways forward in this manner beats hammering it out with emotional exchanges that are laden with defense and accusation.

MANAGE YOUR TRIGGERS WITH T.R.A.I.N.™

Try these steps the next time you are in an inflammatory situation where triggers are heightened and you experience SAFETY conflict.

TRIGGER: Acknowledge your trigger, identify its source, and label your emotion.

REFLECT: Reflect on the SAFETY biases and paradigms that may be influencing your perspective.

APPRAISE: Challenge your negative perspective and consider an alternative, more positive perspective.

INCLUDE: Build in-group connection by taking another's perspective, establish commonalities and increase your exposure to diversity.

NEUTRALIZE: Neutralize your position and language, devoid of unreasonable emotional triggers and engage in an open dialogue that acknowledges the S.A.F.E.T.Y.™ conflict while respecting the psychological safety of all involved.

TEAM SAFETY

With self and relationships sorted out, let's look at the team setting. Recall the research that establishes the link between psychological safety and performance in a team setting.

To recap, members of Psychologically Safe Teams:
- Value psychological safety and are accountable to it
- Protect and nurture the SAFETY of self, relationships, and team
- Harness the strength of the SAFETY diversity of its members
- Promote transparency and openness
- Are not afraid to expose vulnerability or admit mistakes
- Feel safe to take risks or offer opinions

Even with the best intentions, our everyday workplace contexts have the potential to serve or sabotage team psychological safety. Triggers and threats can emerge out of seemingly generic situations.

Team awareness requires perspective-taking from multiple angles. It is the ability to filter operations and activities through a SAFETY lens, entertaining each domain's various biases and perspectives and then anticipating and minimizing potential triggers.

Let's hear from the high-need SAFETY team members to practice team perspective-taking in some common workplace scenarios, and then apply a SAFETY filter to the situation to improve the team's psychological safety. Our characters are:

SAM
Security

AUDREY
Autonomy

FRANK
Fairness

ERIC
Esteem

TRACY
Trust

Learning & Development

The critical role of the brain in a learning setting needs little explanation. Learning requires attention, cognition, and retention, all higher brain functions that rely on an engaged PFC. And of course, excess stress has a negative impact on all of these higher brain functions. It would be counter-productive to set up training initiatives to be threatening, right?

Consider the following communication from Human Resources to the team:

> ### Title: Sexual Harassment Mandatory Training
> *Your attendance is required in Training Room 1 at 9:00 a.m. on Friday, March 4, for a full-day team training workshop on sexual harassment. Attendance is mandatory.*

Brain friendly? What might be potential triggers for our team members?

SAM

"I wish I knew what's being covered and how I'll be expected to participate. What is the motivator behind this training? Is there an issue on the team? Have I done something unknowingly? What if I'm implicated in wrong-doing in this group environment? What would the consequences be? I hope this isn't going to make everything more formal, and change our fun and casual team dynamic. I have a lot of questions and very few answers!"

AUDREY "Really? A whole day, face-to-face? Argh! This is such a waste of my time. I can't stand having these things imposed on me. What about my priorities and freedom of choice? These fixed learning environments with their forced participation in activities and role plays are so tedious. I don't need people telling me how to behave and what's acceptable. For goodness sakes, I'm a grown adult! Here we go with more compliance to another bunch of expectations and rules and measurements."

FRANK "It's so unfair that I'm expected to learn in an environment that doesn't suit my learning style. I know I'm going to be judged against others who thrive in these spaces. And I'm concerned about the lack of consideration for people's sensitivities to such a delicate topic. This could be a very uncomfortable environment for some, and it could put them in a vulnerable position. People who feel vulnerable should be given the opportunity to voice their concerns and not be forced to attend!"

ERIC "Yikes, I'm not up with this topic. I like to be well informed and able to demonstrate my competency to the team. I really hope I'm not called upon for an opinion or to answer a question I don't have the answer to, or worse, be asked to participate in a role play. I hate the idea of my intelligence or performance being exposed, and then judged by everyone. What if my gregarious and fun nature is misinterpreted as sexual harassment and I am shamed in front of the group?"

TRACY "I like the idea of having a full team workshop. We don't get to spend enough time together. I also like that there are going to be parameters established around this topic. We need to be held accountable to group expectations, so we can keep the team strong and cohesive. But I know I think differently than some people on this issue. I have quite traditional values. I'm afraid that I'm not going to fit in, and be labeled as 'unprogressive' and get ostracized and alienated from the group."

With so many considerations, creating a psychologically safe space for every learner is a complex endeavor. If addressed holistically, it could be argued that the way we approach learning, and learning environments, requires a complete rethink and overhaul.

In the meantime, what are some practical and manageable things that could have been done to alleviate the triggers caused by this communication and the pending training?

As a start, consider this communication, filtered for SAFETY:

Title: Compliance Training Notification
As part of management's ongoing commitment to building safe environments, we will be rolling out a series of compliance training topics across the organization over the next 12 months.

The first of these topics is on Sexual Harassment and will be rolled out in the first quarter.

We appreciate that we all have different learning preferences and priorities, and as such we are offering a few options for you to undertake the training by March 31.

Option 1: In-Person Training

This one-day facilitated workshop will be conducted in Training Room 1, 9-5 Friday, March 4, with catering provided. The program will be a combination of presentation and facilitated group discussion where your contribution will be valued but your decision not to share will be respected. A certificate will be awarded upon completion of the open-book compliance training knowledge check, which will be completed either in pairs or individually.

Option 2: Online Modules

This topic is comprised of 6 x 30-minute online modules and knowledge checks. The online option gives you the flexibility to complete the program at your own pace. The program is supported by the option of either online chat forums or video conferencing in peer group pods to digest the learning. A certificate will be awarded upon successful completion of the program requirements.

Prior Learning

There is no prior learning required or expected.

Safe Learning Practices

We are committed to providing you with safe learning environments and promise that we will:
- *promote equity of contribution*
- *discourage group evaluation or critique of your contribution*
- *respect your decision not to share*
- *practice inclusivity and confidentiality*

We appreciate that this topic may be sensitive to some people and encourage you to speak to us privately if you have any concerns or discomfort in participating. We are committed to finding a pathway that works for you.

Can you see how this communication respects SAFETY needs by preempting and addressing potential triggers?

- Provides clarity of purpose, which avoids speculation of motivation
- Takes the guesswork out of the structure and expectations
- Gives individuals choice and control of their learning engagement
- Provides reassurance that nobody will be exposed or put in a vulnerable position
- Sets a tone of inclusion and belonging with options to engage
- Respects equality and personal preferences
- Shows commitment to individuals' safety, privacy, and protection

Change Management

We do not wake up in the morning and hope for instability or disruption. Yet, be it small or transformational, we have had to, and will, experience change in our lives. Change can range from life-changing events like becoming a parent, losing a loved one, or going through a breakup, to transitional events like changing jobs, moving, or changing social circles.

People proceed through phases at different paces, and may experience things differently depending on their context and past. This is where the Y (You) in SAFETY becomes critical. The magnitude of change varies, but the scale of change is not as important as the way in which we manage the process. It is helpful to understand what is happening in the brain throughout.

Consider this scenario:

After months of rumors and speculation, the team has just had it confirmed through the gossip chain that the company will be undergoing a significant restructure. It seems management has made the decision at a conceptual level, but there is very little information about the details and the potential impacts. Of course, there will be changes to teams and roles. It may even mean redundancies and layoffs. This bombshell has annihilated the team's psychological safety landscape and has left in its wake chaos and trepidation as everyone scrambles to understand what this means for them, what the impact on their lives might be, and what their next moves should be.

Let's take a peek into the inner dialogue of the team members as they wrestle with their fears and insecurities.

SAM "My world is falling apart. I have no security, and there is no semblance of consistency, certainty, or clarity. I don't know what this means for me and my future, and nobody has any details. I have nowhere to turn. Everybody is in the same situation. There is no 'rock' to hold onto, no process to follow, or proven formula on how to get through this. There are no safety rails."

AUDREY "I have lost total control over my life. I am at the mercy of others who are making decisions about my future, irrespective of my wants and needs. I have no choices. They will decide if I stay or go, what my role will be, who my team will be."

FRANK "How can they make this decision without any consultation? This is so wrong. We should have been given a voice in this process. Doesn't my loyalty, hard work, and sacrifice count for anything around here? Will it even be considered in the final wash? Their lack of communication and the lack of transparency of the process are completely unjust. These are our lives they are playing with!"

ERIC "What if they decide I am not valuable? Right now I have the title and the office to prove that I am, but that could all change in a heartbeat. I have a reputation for being the decision-maker and influencer around here, what will people think if I get demoted or laid off? What if I end up unemployed and can't get another job? What if I lose my house and my car? There goes all my status and credibility."

TRACY "I don't know who I can trust any more. Who is on my side? Who will be loyal? Who are the decision makers? I don't know if people will betray me to protect their own interests, or if they have my back and will fight for me. These people have become like family. Not being a part of this team would be crushing."

The team leader, although gripped with his own insecurities and fears, recognizes his team's pain and knows they are looking to him for answers and for cues on how to respond. He understands that he can't give them a lot of what they are looking for right now. What he can do is focus on their psychological safety, and so he leads them through a T.R.A.I.N.™ process to help them deal with their triggers and fears.

He has them:

- Identify their triggers and label their emotions.
- Reflect on their inner dialogue and what it reveals about their fears, categorizing those into real or perceived threats. Are the fears justified in light of what we know about the change so far, or are they based on speculation?
- Consider other interpretations of the situation. Are there any potential positives, large or small? Is there a best-case scenario?
- Build on the commonalities of the team, their shared experiences, their shared fears and emotions.
- Engage in an open and transparent discussion about a pathway forward. What tangible actions can team members take to minimize their triggers and appeal to their SAFETY needs?

Can you see how this process nurtures psychological safety amid uncertainty?

- Acknowledges and validates their fears and anxiety
- Allows their voices to be heard
- Reassures them that they are not alone
- Allows them to entertain alternative, less-negative perspectives
- Models openness and transparency
- Evokes empathy for the shared experience of the group
- Gives a sense of control by having a tangible way forward
- Shows commitment to their safety and well-being

Onboarding

The onboarding experience is full of opportunities to get SAFETY right, or really wrong.

The restructure changes have now been confirmed. The good news is all members will be retaining their jobs. The sad news is their happy little team will be dissolved and the members repositioned in other teams in various locations. Because they were a unique, highly autonomous team, the members had developed their own culture and played by their own rules. For them, this change is like moving to a brand new company. They are leaving a familiar environment where they know who's who, how things operate, and what is expected of them. They built deep personal friendships and partnerships. They knew all the backstories, the routines, and the physical landscape.

Now, everything is new and unfamiliar. They don't know anyone or any of the unwritten rules, and they're not part of the inside jokes or culture. Their team is disbanded on a Friday and each member is given the location and the name of their new manager. They are to commence on their new teams on Monday.

Let's look at how our bruised and battered SAFETY characters are coping with this upheaval.

SAM

"I am lost. Everything that was familiar is gone, and I'm faced with overwhelming uncertainty, inconsistency, and lack of clarity amidst a mountain of change. My daily routines have been deconstructed: where to go, what to do, who to see. I don't know the processes, and I am not clear on the expectations of my role. I don't know who to turn to or how to get things done."

AUDREY

"I feel like I have totally lost control over my life. I have less freedom to decide how I spend my day and have to look to others for guidance and direction. I hate having to rely on other people while I learn the ropes. Now I have to educate a new team on how I like to work and be managed. If this new team culture doesn't provide the same autonomy I'm used to, I am really going to struggle."

FRANK "I feel like I am really on the back foot, I don't have a good sense of my role and I really don't know what I don't know. I don't know how they expect me to compete on a level playing field or integrate into this new team when they have not been transparent about my new role. This whole process has been a disgrace. Nobody's needs have been considered. There's been no consultation on a change that has significant impacts on our lives. The fact that it was our team that got dissolved, not the sales team, really highlights the politics and preferential treatment rife in this organization."

ERIC "I feel awkward and unknown. I don't know where I fit and don't feel valued or highly regarded. No one understands the skills, experience, and abilities I bring to the table. I was really 'someone' on the old team; I had the office and the title and the status. I was respected and people really valued my contribution. Now I am a nobody. I don't feel comfortable speaking up or offering opinions until I get a better read on this team and their position on things. I feel like I've fallen from the top of the food chain. Now I have to build my way back up from the bottom."

TRACY "I feel isolated and alienated. I don't yet understand the new group dynamics, and I'm not sure how to make my way into the fold. I haven't made any real connections or built rapport. I don't know where I belong. I loved the old team. We were like family, we all looked after one another and respected our differences. We shared the same sense of humor and had our own in-group banter. That's all gone now, and I feel like a stranger on the periphery."

Let's replay this transition with a SAFETY-sensitive approach.

- Management communicates the pending change, the reason for it and the benefits, and expresses genuine acknowledgment and concern for the significant personal impact of transition on the team members.
- The team commemorates their achievements with a farewell dinner. Members are acknowledged for their contribution, and the team shares memories and stories of their time together.
- Each team member has a one-on-one session with extensive details about their new role and team, and is allocated coach support for the change process.
- Members are sent a personal congratulation email from the leader of their new group, welcoming them and introducing the new team. The email provides all the information they need for their first day, along with their first week's schedule, and links to useful documents, photos, sites, or videos that will orient them to the landscape and culture of their new team.
- An assigned "buddy" on the new team checks in on them over the next few days and makes an effort to get to know their likes/dislikes, hobbies, and interests, and connects them with others on the team that have common interests.

- On their first day, the new members are met by the full team in the lobby. Their workspace has welcome signs from the new team, and their assigned buddy acts as their personal guide and companion throughout the day and continues to support them throughout their first few weeks.
- Human Resources takes an active role in the member's onboarding and follows up with phone calls on day 2, day 7, day 14, and day 30 to see how they are settling in and to offer support.

Can you see how these simple changes to the experience might dampen the threat response and make for a more smooth, welcoming, and enjoyable transition? The process:
- Provides details and support at each step
- Gives generous space for inquiry and familiarization
- Acknowledges, validates, and celebrates members' contributions
- Recognizes the importance and meaning of an ending
- Celebrates and ritualizes belonging and transition
- Provides reassurance and companionship
- Models openness, warmth, and transparency
- Provides a sense of choice and control
- Ensures ongoing commitment to everyone's safety and well-being

Performance Discussions

You don't need to be an expert to know that performance reviews are a situation full of potential SAFETY triggers and amygdala reactions. There are many adjustments that can be made to the Performance Review process through the lens of SAFETY. You may even question the efficacy of the whole process. That said, even small adjustments can improve the effectiveness of the discussion. And the discussion is the heart of the process.

Let's check in on our team members.

Nearing the end of the first year in their new teams, the members are asked to write their self-reviews. They dig deep to justify their value and contribution to the organization over the past year. They have worked hard and had their share of wins, all in the face of adversity, but was it enough? They submit their summaries, then wait two months to get the final verdict of how their work stacked up against that of others over the prior year.

Perfect environment for our SAFETY characters to get very vocal.

SAM "I know how I performed, and I have the data to support it, but I don't have the data about those I am being measured against. I have no idea how the evaluation is being done. Not only am I uncertain about the data and process, I have no certainty or security about what the outcome might mean for me. Will I be demoted? Will I even have a job at the end of this?"

AUDREY

 "I hate being told what to do and how to do it, and this process is just that. I respond best when

I invite input and feedback, not when it is imposed on me. This case is the complete opposite. I am told when to show up to hear what I did well and where I fell short and what I could do to improve. And then I'll be forced to set my goals and be told how I will be tracked and measured."

FRANK 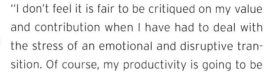 "I don't feel it is fair to be critiqued on my value and contribution when I have had to deal with the stress of an emotional and disruptive transition. Of course, my productivity is going to be impacted as I get settled and deal with the change! Will they account for that? How? I know I haven't performed at my optimum, and I don't think it's fair to be measured against the same criteria as people who are firmly established. They have history, they have stronger relationships and rapport, and they've had more opportunity and resources and support than I have."

ERIC "This is such a bittersweet ride for me. On the one hand, if it goes well, I'm very excited about being validated and getting the accolades and acknowledgement that will follow. I like to know that I have performed well in comparison to others. It'll help me gauge if I am making progress on working my way back up the food chain. On the other hand, I'll be devastated if it doesn't go well and my status is challenged. What if I fall short of expectations and my performance is criticized? It will be so humiliating to know that others are aware of my inadequacies and to be judged for them."

TRACY "Being relatively new, I am still unsure about my relationship with my boss. There are decision-makers in this process that I don't know, and I am nervous about the peer feedback they received from my new teammates. I'm still not fully immersed. It's taking a long time to integrate into the team and culture. I hope I can trust the relationships I have built so far. They're still in their infancy, and I don't know yet if these people embrace me or appreciate my value. I'm not sure I can depend on their loyalty."

Creating a situation free from all triggers in this process is nothing short of impossible. However, let's consider this process with a SAFETY-sensitive approach.

Understanding that the new team members are fragile after dealing with the upheaval of change and transition, the team leader is mindful that they may be particularly SAFETY sensitive around performance review time. Thankfully, because performance issues and feedback have been addressed as necessary throughout the year, this end-of-year conference can be an opportunity to summarize what has already been discussed, and wrap up by aligning on the upcoming year.

To help set the tone for a psychologically safe experience and to dial down potential triggers, the leader takes the opportunity to reassure members that the performance review is not going to be a surprise of unexpected feedback and performance critique. He or she offers a process that helps cater to the members' SAFETY drivers.

"Congratulations on completing your first year on the team. Thank you for your contribution and hard work. I know it hasn't been a particularly comfortable

year for you, and watching you overcome and embrace the challenge has been inspirational.

"As we wrap up the year, I would love to get together and summarize what we have discussed throughout the year, and plan for the year ahead. I am excited about starting next year strongly, and this is an opportunity to consolidate our thinking and align on priorities.

"Here are a few things that will help facilitate that process:

1. *To inform the discussion I would love to hear your perspective on a few things. The details are outlined on the form attached. It would be great if you could complete it and email it back to me in the next two weeks.*
2. *Can you carve out a couple of hours in the first or second week of December for us to catch up? Send me a meeting request.*
2. *This is an informal discussion, so feel free to choose a location that works best for you: in your office, at a restaurant, or even taking a stroll works for me. I'll leave it up to you.*

"If you have any questions or concerns, please don't hesitate to reach out. Thanks for your partnership. I am really looking forward to catching up."

See how this lays a foundation for a safe discussion?

- Identification of the challenges faced and overcome
- Encouragement and acknowledgement of contribution

- Creation of trust and in-group with casual language and approach
- Reassurance that there will be no big surprises
- Freedom over when and where the discussion takes place
- Security about what to expect
- Generous approach to deliverables and support

Feedback or Feedsmack?

Feedback (or feedsmack) is no friend of the brain, especially feedback that is imposed rather than invited. Let's look at the scenario a bit differently this time and see how each domain is impacted when Joe receives the following statement from the team manager on a Thursday afternoon.

Hi Joe, I have some feedback for you about the meeting we were just in. Let's the two of us discuss it next Tuesday at 2:00 in my office.

Innocent? Free from SAFETY triggers? Let's break it down.

SECURITY: "I have no sense of Security about what is happening next Tuesday at 2:00. I don't know what to expect, or even if I will have a job after next Tuesday at 2:00."

AUTONOMY: "Where is my choice in this? I was not asked if next Tuesday at 2:00 is a good date or time for me, or even if I was interested in discussing the meeting or receiving feedback."

FAIRNESS: "What is she not telling me? It is completely unfair to drop that bomb and leave me in the dark until next Tuesday. Why is it just me getting feedback? What about the others in the meeting?"

ESTEEM: "What did I do in the meeting? Did I do something to offend her? Is she upset with me? I'm feeling completely vulnerable and exposed right now."

TRUST: "I thought we had come a long way and built rapport in our relationship, but I am now questioning if she really has my back. I don't know if I can trust her, given that communication."

With a seemingly simple comment, this manager has triggered every SAFETY motivator. In one fell swoop, the amygdala has been activated on all levels, severely compromising access to the PFC. Between now and next Tuesday at 2:00, the manager can be assured that Joe will experience severely limited productivity and creativity. His critical thinking will be diminished and his perspective narrowed. In fact, the manager will be lucky if Joe regains his full cognitive ability on Tuesday at 3:00. It is likely there will be residual impact for some time.

Let's replay the situation with a replacement memo that may minimize the amygdala response.

Hi Joe. I would love to hear your thoughts or insights from that meeting. No urgency. Let me know when would be a good time to catch you, and I will stop by.

Feedback is challenging to address. It is full of complexities, emotion, and nuance. In this simple rephrase, the manager:

- Prioritizes Joe's thoughts and insights as the basis for discussion
- Is casual and flexible in her approach, rather than urgent and demanding
- Implies partnership and collaboration
- Implies equity in the exchange rather than a one-way communication
- Gives choice on when and where the discussion takes place
- Sets a non-threatening stage for feedback to be delivered safely

The Call to Creativity

We are often challenged to be creative and innovative in high-pressured environments that are anything but brain friendly.

Innovation and creativity require heavy brain power and an environment conducive to insight. Specifically, stress interferes with our creativity potential, so setting the right conditions to have brains in a threat-free state is critical. There is nothing more unhelpful to innovation than an amygdala hijack.

Let's look at the impact on a team's SAFETY when they receive this note from their Head of Innovation:

Hi Team,
Management have brought forward the deadline to submit our annual product strategy, complete with implementation timelines, to next Friday. Needless

to say, it is creativity and innovation time! Come prepared with your ideas to our brainstorming session in the conference room on Tuesday at 2:00 p.m. Attendance is mandatory.

Bring your thinking caps and snacks as we won't be leaving the room until we are done—it could be a long night! Look forward to seeing you then.

A little extreme, perhaps. However, it is not uncommon to have unreasonable goals imposed on us, under tough conditions, where we are expected to bring our best thinking.

Let's hear from the team members.

SAM "What should I do to prepare? What do they expect from me? What is the background on new products being considered? I wonder what process will be used to get all this done in such a short time. Speaking of time, there is not even an indication of when the meeting might end. Do I bring dinner? Could it go all night? Do I arrange for an overnight babysitter?"

AUDREY "How can they insist on mandatory participation with an open-ended finish time? This whole situation is outrageous. There is no consideration of whether this is something I want to be involved with. I know I don't do my best creative thinking collectively. I am much better on my own."

FRANK "What they are imposing on us completely violates fair work practice. Mandating that we work into the night without even providing meals is disgusting. What if I had other priorities or commitments for that time? It's unfair that we are penalized because management changed the deadline."

ERIC "I hate brainstorming sessions. What if I can't come up with good ideas, or worse, any ideas? What if my ideas look stupid compared to others? I will be so humiliated if my ideas are met with eye rolls, ridicule, or rejection."

TRACY "I think I'm happy to be invited. I guess it means I am considered part of the team. But I'm nervous about the group dynamics. I'm still unsure how I fit in and whether the team will embrace me and my ideas. Or will I be the awkward character who sits on their own and doesn't get included?"

Now for a psychological safety approach where innovation is more likely to succeed:

Hi Team,
Okay, I have been thrown a tricky curveball that I am going to need your help to navigate.
  Due to unforeseen changes in governance compliance deadlines, management is required to have all annual plans submitted by the end of the month. They

are very apologetic and understand this puts additional pressure on an already crazy schedule, but they are requesting our annual product strategy report be submitted in two weeks.

I know this seems impossible, but I have come up with a process I hope respects you and your time in order to get the job done. I welcome any further ideas or improvements.

Rather than the traditional approach of bunkering down for hours or days in a brain-unfriendly brainstorming session, I propose we divide and conquer and use a combination of individual and group work to tackle this.

STEP 1

Process: To help generate the best ideas, I would like you all to find a time that suits you over the next 48 hours, do your thinking, and jot down your ideas. Be as creative and wild with your input as possible. It is often in the outrageous that we stumble upon genius.

Logistics: Please submit ideas to me by email by 12 noon on Wednesday, and indicate if your preference is for anonymity.

STEP 2

Process: I will present these, collated and chunked for processing, at two half-day sessions. We will not be critiquing individual ideas but will be using a group voting process to refine the ideas and find consensus.

Logistics: *We will make use of our best morning brains on Thursday and Friday, from 8-12. Hopefully this requires less juggling of schedules than a full-day session at such late notice. Breakfast, morning refreshments, and lunch will be provided.*

STEP 3

Process: *Depending where we get to by midday Friday, we may need to assign individuals or subgroups to work on particular aspects of the plan next week. So please free up your schedule next week where you can.*

Logistics: *Friday 12 p.m. we will evaluate where we are and decide as a group if it makes sense to continue working for the rest of the day for those who are available.*

Please let me know if you have questions or concerns about your involvement in this process, and we can work together to ensure that your valuable contribution is captured.

Once again, I deeply appreciate your partnership in this, I don't know what I would do without you.

So how does this approach appeal to SAFETY and set up a better dynamic for creativity and innovation? The approach:

- Is empathetic and apologetic and acknowledges the imposition
- Provides details about context and process
- Appeals to the camaraderie and solidarity of the group
- Acknowledges the value of individual contribution and commitment

- Gives flexibility and choice throughout the process
- Is sensitive to members' status and privacy needs

The Social Dynamic

We have all experienced that enthusiastic team member who takes on her volunteer role as the team's social club coordinator with gusto. Let's call her Mary and peek in on her activities.

Passionate and energetic about building team rapport, Mary is bursting with excitement about this year's team social calendar. She has carefully coordinated it with Human Resources. It's taken weeks to engineer a range of fun and diverse events for the team to enjoy. From team-building activities to birthday celebrations and social gatherings, she has it covered. There is something for everyone. Mary is surprised that the team doesn't express more enthusiasm when they find a year's worth of functions populating their calendars and a plethora of invitations filling their inboxes.

Not so surprising for many of us. Can you empathize with our characters' responses?

SAM "How are these events going to play out? I like to know what I am in for. I don't want to be put in social situations that put pressure on me to do things that push me out of my comfort zone, like karaoke or dancing. What if I am pressured to do risky activities like rock climbing or zip-lining in one of these team building activities?"

AUDREY "This is crazy. How dare she populate my already full calendar with all these events? She knows I don't like having my schedule dictated to me or be pressured to commit to events and activities in advance. She just never lets up!"

FRANK "Is involvement in all of this going to come at my personal expense? Nights out, cards, cakes, presents, that's a lot of expectation, and it makes assumptions about people's financial position. I want to know how they will ensure equity and fairness when it comes to birthday celebrations and gifts!"

ERIC "This schedule is littered with ego threats. Just like last year when Frank received a much more expensive present and double the attendance at his celebration than I did. It just highlighted how much more liked he is. And I don't do well with physical activities, so the humiliation of not being able to climb the rock wall, or losing every race at the team building exercise, does not thrill me."

TRACY "I never know if people will include me or if I'll end up awkwardly sitting alone. I'm not sporty like everyone else. I don't know if I'll be picked for teams on team-building day, or be left as the 'last-woman-standing.' I can see myself as the rejected person nobody wanted."

Maybe a more toned-down approach would have had a more positive response.

Hi Team,

As part of our commitment to find ways to build team rapport and connection, I wanted to give you access to an outline of events, celebrations, and activities for the year. Please find a pdf attached with the annual calendar.

Out of respect for full schedules and inboxes we will be not be populating these into the team calendar, so you may like to review the activities and events attached and add those to your personal calendar that interest you.

To take out the guess–work, please find below the outline of process and expectations around involvement in the various activities.

Birthdays

- *A birthday email will go out on behalf of the team, with the full team cc'd. This will serve as a reminder and a prompt to respond with birthday wishes.*
- *During the morning break you are welcome to join us for cake and presentation of a card and $50 gift voucher. No financial contribution is required.*
- *To simplify things, celebrations outside of this will not be facilitated at a team level. Organization and*

attendance at additional celebrations will be completely voluntary.

Team Socials
- *Once a quarter we will hold a casual team social as an opportunity to connect and have some well-earned fun.*
- *An email invitation with logistics, attire, and associated costs will go out a month prior, and RSVPs will close 2 weeks prior.*
- *Of course, we would love to see you all, but there is no obligation to attend.*

Team Building
- *We will have two organization-funded team-building activities this year.*
- *Although your choice not to participate in particular activities during the day is respected, we do request that all members attend if only for support.*
- *These two events will be populated in the team calendar to serve as reminders.*
- *More details will be sent via email one month out.*

Thanks everyone! Please let me know if you have any suggestions or feedback on the plan or the events.

This might seem like excessive communication for a social calendar, but in one email the entire year's expectations and rules of engagement are set up.

In this process and communication, the team are supported with:
- Respect for their time, their needs, and their resources
- Clarity of process, details, and expectations

- Equity in process and treatment
- Freedom of choice in how and when they engage
- Opportunities to be acknowledged and included

Recognition & Reward

Sometimes initiatives can have the best intentions but can backfire badly.

> *HR has just introduced a new recognition and reward program that includes an online acknowledgment system in which every staff member is enrolled and is expected to participate. The system is designed to be transparent, and as such everyone has access to the acknowledgments and recognition that people have both given and received. This is a great idea that is going to give a forum for people's contribution to be valued and highlighted. The feedback on the forum will be a contributing factor to monthly and annual awards, and data will be reviewed as part of the annual performance review process.*

In theory, this seems a great reward-triggering system. However, look how our SAFETY team finds it underpinned with significant psychological sabotage:

SAM "What are the rules of engagement? What are we supposed to do? How much should I acknowledge others, and how much should I expect to be acknowledged? What sorts of things should I acknowledge? If this is a contributing factor to how I am going to be rewarded and how my performance will be reviewed, I need to know how the data is evaluated."

AUDREY "I don't like the automatic enrollment and expectation to engage with this system. I want to acknowledge people when and how I like, not have it imposed. I don't like that I have no control over what others see when it comes to what acknowledgements I give and receive."

FRANK "How does this system account for roles like mine that are more in the background with no direct reporting to management? There is no equity in this process. The nature of my role means that people don't see my impact or the value I bring. Add to that the fact that I work independently rather than in a team, and it means people are not exposed to my wins and achievements and won't acknowledge them."

ERIC "It is so obvious that sales VPs are more highly valued than other roles in the organization. They get all the acknowledgment from senior management for keeping the business afloat. Meanwhile, those of us supporting and enabling them to succeed are ignored, only receiving acknowledgment from peers and subordinates."

TRACY "This system is just one big butt-kissing and popularity contest. People will use the opportunity to acknowledge those in their in-group, and neglect to acknowledge those not in their clique. The system is so biased. It ensures that in-group members are protected and rewarded, and those in the out-group are ignored and punished."

Yikes, not sounding like a very rewarding experience at this point.

So is there a way to do this that would be more SAFETY sensitive?

Our suggestion in this case would be to have a more structured and meaningful approach to a recognition and reward system, rather than an ad hoc approach. Some suggestions would be to establish a culture that:

- Practices giving meaningful and generous feedback
- Knows and respects each individual's personal acknowledgment preferences
- Ensures fairness and equity in acknowledgment both in quantity and weight
- Systemizes and prompts acknowledgment to ensure people are not overlooked
- Celebrates team success as the sum total of its contributors
- Is transparent in its recognition and reward process

CULTURAL SAFETY

Given the importance of psychological safety for well-being, relationships, and performance, our cultures are well served by nurturing and protecting their population's psychological safety in the same way as its physical safety.

Recall that culture is what endorses, promotes, and standardizes the expectations and rules around psychological safety. The accountability set and monitored at this systemic level truly empowers psychological safety at the other three levels.

Let's look at the cultural characteristics, the population experience, and the key areas of responsibility for building psychologically safe cultures.

Cultural Characteristics

Recall that psychologically safe cultures:

- Value and promote psychological safety as a cultural standard
- Speak a common SAFETY language
- Protect psychological safety through policy, process, and practice

- Are accountable to the psychological safety standards and expectations

Cultural Experience

In environments where psychological safety is endorsed at the macro level, people feel:
- Valued and respected
- Appreciated and heard
- Empowered to be transparent and open
- Safe to expose vulnerability or admit mistakes
- Safe to take risks or offer opinions
- Equipped to express their SAFETY needs
- Committed to supporting other's SAFETY needs
- Confident that their psychological safety is protected and supported

Cultural Responsibility

- Advocacy
- Language
- Expectation
- Accountability

ADVOCACY

Advocacy is about exposure, education, and expectations. When done well, the population will recognize and understand psychological safety, know what they can expect and what is expected of them, and identify psychological safety as a workplace priority.

From our experience, cultural transformation happens one brain at a time. Hence our recommendation to build psychological safety from the grass roots of "self." As such it makes sense to start with education that promotes self-awareness. Understanding psychological safety and what it means at a personal level is a critical first step to promoting awareness and adoption. This baseline understanding can be leveraged to influence relationships, then the team, and finally the wider context of culture.

LANGUAGE

Common language is often a key attribute of a defined culture. Speaking a common language better facilitates people's ability to identify with, articulate, comprehend, and communicate ideas and concepts.

The ability to communicate your needs, comprehend others' needs, and manage expectations, is much easier when we are all speaking the same language.

Adopting a framework and language for psychological safety can help people personally identify with the concepts, as well as establish a common understanding that improves our ability to relate and communicate.

EXPECTATION

An authentic commitment to psychological safety at the cultural level requires the same systemic focus as we see for other occupational safety and health (OSHA) risk factors. Language, values, behaviors, and rules are defined at this macro level. It is about setting tone and expectations.

When a culture is psychologically safe, it uses SAFETY as a filter for policies and procedure, decisions and communications, conduct and language, measurement and reporting.

People in psychologically safe cultures know what they can expect, what is expected from them, and can rely on the systems and infrastructure to support them and protect their interests.

ACCOUNTABILITY

Advocacy, language, and expectations all facilitate awareness and adoption, and are great steps in the right direction. However, these are not enough in and of themselves. In fact, if we are not careful, creating this awareness can backfire.

When psychological safety is identified and embraced as a cultural priority, it must be reinforced with accountability. Implementing the first three steps creates an informed army of individuals who will critique the integrity of the organization's commitment to psychological safety when they evaluate their experience against the established expectations.

If people are told that psychological safety is valued and a priority, they will be looking for consistency between what is espoused and what is practiced. A disconnect between the espoused value and their experience can sabotage SAFETY efforts and trigger an even stronger threat response, as it can be perceived as willful negligence.

Accountability is where the rubber hits the road and where theory turns into practice. A cultural commitment to psychological safety is only as strong as the commitment the organization makes to holding itself and its members accountable. Being diligent about compliance with policy, metrics, tracking, reporting, and repercussions for noncompliance is pivotal.

NOW WHAT?

So where to from here? Let's break this down in sequence.

There is no magic pill that will eradicate psychological triggers from your life or prevent you from pushing others' SAFETY buttons. However, becoming aware of your drivers and how they may manifest in your behaviors and motivations is a great start to understanding psychological safety.

The best way to do this is by taking the SAFETY assessment. Understanding your profile and how it might be manifesting for you and others will give you a new way to understand your needs, and a new language to express them.

You can also look for clues about how you are driven by starting to notice the subtleties of your internal world—your judgments, opinions, perspectives, attitudes, and beliefs.

Remember, you are not looking for a determination of right or wrong. Everyone has a background story that has shaped their brain's wiring. Although your brain maps may be outdated and in need of renewal with respect to some contexts, these filters were created in your best interests.

As you become more self-aware, and understand your nonconscious drivers, you become more empathetic, compassionate, and forgiving of yourself and of others, because, after all, "it's not you, it's your brain." This paves the way for healthier relationships and more supportive environments that contribute to better performance and collaboration.

We encourage you to become more attentive to your environment. How is your psychological safety influenced and even manipulated by the world around you? You only have to look at the nature of marketing, media, entertainment, and politics to see how SAFETY drivers are used to influence your thinking and decisions, rewarding your drivers by appealing to your importance, belonging, security, freedom, or equality.

Or, more commonly, these outlets trigger you by highlighting a violation or threat to your drivers. As we have established, a threat to the brain has far more impact than a reward, so appealing to your fears is a powerful way to get your attention, fire you up, and enlist your support.

You can go a long way to creating more psychologically safe environments by becoming self-aware and taking personal responsibility for how you are impacted and how you impact others.

SELF

STEP 1

Take the S.A.F.E.T.Y.™ Assessment and reflect on the results

You might find it helpful to discuss your report with an accredited coach to generate the most insights about your views:

- How is your SAFETY being protected or rewarded by holding those views?
- How are those views helping you or serving you?
- How might they be unhelpful to you or sabotaging you?
- How might those views be threatening or rewarding the psychological safety of others?

STEP 2

Develop your sensitivity and manage your triggers

Be conscious of how you are experiencing situations and use the T.R.A.I.N.™ process to:

- Catch and label your triggers
- Reflect on your biases and perception
- Challenge your assumptions and conclusions
- Reinterpret the situation with a S.A.F.E.T.Y.™ lens and adopt an in-group mindset

RELATIONSHIP

In some relationships you may feel like you are doing your best to meet the needs of the other person, yet you continue to miss the mark and can't seem to get it right. This can cause frustration and even resentment when your good intentions and efforts seem to be in vain.

It is easy to fall victim to the false consensus bias, which has us believing that others think the same way that we do. The idea of treating others the way you want to be treated is suggested by the Golden Rule: "Do unto others as you would have them do unto you."

However, neuroscience research tells us that no two brains are mapped exactly the same. We should not be applying the Golden Rule, but rather the Platinum rule: "Treat others the way they want to be treated."

By applying your rules to others rather than their rules, your efforts are likely to have either no effect, or even trigger them in a negative way. You will have more success in your relationships if you take the time to understand the psychological triggers of others and work to avoid threatening their safety.

Even if it is unintentional, at some point you will trigger one of the important domains for someone. The key is to recognize when that happens, and diffuse. That might sound like this: "It looks like I may have triggered your Fairness domain. Let me give you some context to why that decision was made."

This simple statement could be enough to open a healthy dialogue with others and minimize the intensity of the trigger's effect on the PFC. In addition, it propagates a common language, which helps foster an in-group perception.

Of course, prevention is better than cure, so taking steps to understand others' profiles and needs up-front is the best starting point. Educate yourself on their needs and any gaps in how you are relating. Consider taking the S.A.F.E.T.Y.™ Assessment and reviewing your profiles together to get on the same page and begin to understand each other's paradigms.

Conversely, sharing what the other could do to nurture *your* psychological safety can help them understand your needs and guide discussions that look at strategies and agreements moving forward.

These transparent discussions take the assumptions and guesswork out of relationships, and cut through that "old brain" temptation to jump to conclusions and judge motivations. Not only will this shed light on how to get the best thinking from each other, it will also help build the Trust domain between the two of you.

RELATIONSHIP

STEP 1

Get on the Same Page

You might find it helpful to discuss your report with an accredited coach to generate the most insights about your views:

- Learn about each other's drivers and triggers. Use your SAFETY reports to facilitate a discussion on how your profiles differ.
- What behaviors or assumptions have you made in the past that, unknowingly, may have triggered them, and you?
- Share how you can both best nurture each other's psychological safety and protect each other's triggers.

STEP 2

Protect Each Other's SAFETY

Use the T.R.A.I.N.™ process to manage triggers and resolve conflict with psychological safety as the goal.

TEAM

Research suggests that psychological safety is a critical factor for a successful team. By understanding the SAFETY hierarchy for each person in your team, you can gain insights into how to work with each individual to protect their psychological safety and keep them in the best mental state for higher thinking and performance.

The more you understand the SAFETY domains, the better you will identify what might trigger someone in a given situation. One of the best ways to quickly understand each person on your team is to have them take the S.A.F.E.T.Y.™ Assessment and then have a team discussion about the findings.

To take this to a deeper level and really understand and build team psychological safety, engage an accredited facilitator to take the team through a S.A.F.E.T.Y.™ Team Debrief Workshop to increase their SAFETY awareness of themselves, of each other, and of the overall team. Equip them with the knowledge and skills they need to understand and express their SAFETY needs, to increase their sensitivity to and protection of each other's needs, and to appreciate the diversity of strengths and challenges in the team's SAFETY profile.

TEAM

STEP 1

Understand Your Team's SAFETY

Use member SAFETY profiles to engage in a team discussion. Questions to consider as you discuss the team's profiles:

- In what ways do our profiles strengthen one another?
- In what ways might our profiles interfere with the team's performance?
- How can we use this as a language within the team to inform someone when we are feeling triggered?

For a richer experience, engage an accredited facilitator to conduct a S.A.F.E.T.Y.™ Team Debrief Workshop to equip members with knowledge and skills to build psychological safety for themselves and others.

STEP 2

Adopt a SAFETY Lens

Become sensitive to how situations, communications, activities, and behaviors may impact particular SAFETY drivers in the team. Use SAFETY to filter for triggers and modify language and behavior as necessary to minimize impact.

CULTURE

As microcosms of our broader cultures, and because they stand to benefit greatly from improved productivity and performance, our workplace cultures are a logical starting point to begin the important work of instituting psychological safety. Unlike with many things in this world, there is no loser with psychological safety. In this unique paradigm, the organization's drive for the bottom line does not come at the expense of its people's best interests.

In organizations with psychologically safe cultures, everyone wins. Their people stand to improve their productivity, well-being, and relationships. Their teams, and by default the organization as a whole, reap the benefits of improved performance and results.

CULTURE

STEP 1

Identify Psychological Safety as a Cultural Priority

Recognize the solid business case for adopting a psychological safety approach to operations.

STEP 2

Implement Psychological Safety Across the Population

- Advocacy: education and promotion
- Language: framework and language
- Expectation: policies and procedures
- Accountability: measurement and reporting

THE S.A.F.E.T.Y.™ ASSESSMENT

We have developed an online assessment that provides a detailed report of how your brain responds to the various S-A-F-E-T domains. You'll notice that we only cover the first five components of the acronym due to the fact that the "Y" is so incredibly complex and variable between individuals. Unless we included extensive genetic and biological testing, along with intensive psychotherapy in the assessment, we wouldn't do the "Y" justice. The philosophy behind this assessment is that by gaining self-awareness of your motivational drivers, you can better manage your performance and collaborate more efficiently with others.

Background

The S.A.F.E.T.Y.™ Assessment is a validated tool that ranks and quantifies how important the five social triggers are to you individually. A simple online questionnaire asks about your preferences and attitudes toward everyday situations related to the S.A.F.E.T. domains, and takes approximately 15 minutes to complete.

For each question, you are asked what importance you attach to that topic, on a scale of 0 to 10. Your average score of the 10 questions in each domain (raw score) is calculated and then, for context, compared to the thousands of other people who have taken the assessment. Your score in each domain is represented as a percentile and indicates your relative sensitivity to the domain.

The results from the assessment are designed to assist you in creating self-awareness around what drives your motivation, and the relative importance of all the domains to you individually. The assessment report also identifies how you might experience threats in each domain and how other people might experience your behavior.

Your Turn

Your turn. Stop here and take the assessment. Familiarize yourself with your results.

To take the assessment, visit www.ablsafety.com. You can complete the assessment and receive your top domain for free. However, this is only part of the story. Your two highest domains along with your lowest domain are the key drivers of your behavior. To receive a comprehensive report, either purchase a code at www.ablsafety.com prior to taking the assessment, or simply upgrade after completing the assessment.

Validity

The generation of questions for the assessment required considerable pilot work during its development. Wording and content were refined and the questions were revised over multiple rounds of review to ensure that the items reflected content adequacy.

To assure content validity, the questions were generated from a number of sources, including consultation with experts in the field, proposed respondents, and review of associated literature.

Consideration was given to the order in which items were presented. The acquiescent response bias (i.e. the tendency for respondents to agree with a statement or respond in the same way to successive items) was addressed by incorporating a mixture of both positively and negatively worded items.

Understanding Your Assessment

It is important to note that this assessment is not a personality sorter. It is not an indicator of your personality style or a test for any of the widely used personality dimensions.

Rather, the S.A.F.E.T.Y.™ Assessment provides an outline of how your brain is motivated in your current context, thus suggesting how quickly or easily you may be triggered by each domain.

It can be easy to fall into the trap of assuming that one domain is better than another. This is absolutely not the case. Every one of us is motivated by all five of the SAFETY domains. We all seek Security, Autonomy, Fairness, Esteem, and Trust in our lives, and we have all been, and will continue to be, triggered by each domain. Even your lowest-rated domain will trigger a lower brain (amygdala) response at some point.

For example, if Esteem is your lowest domain, this does not mean that you are not motivated by Esteem. It simply means that your personal experiences up to this point, as well as your current context, allow your brain to have a slightly longer Esteem fuse before triggering your amygdala.

In addition, it is important to remember that all five of the domains are linked. Using the example above, if Esteem is your fifth domain and Fairness is your first, an act of unfairness may set off your need for Fairness, which could in turn set off your need for Esteem, creating a multiplier effect and an even larger amygdala response.

Understanding the details of your assessment may require you to go back and re-read the previous chapters. Each of the domains is full of nuance and research details, and each of us is driven to some extent by all five domains. It is important to understand the interaction between them and to learn what part of each domain is likely to be your trigger point.

FINAL WORD

This is just the beginning. We have only scratched the surface of the world of psychological safety. Over time, we look forward to building on this introduction and diving more deeply into various topics and contexts. With research still in its infancy, the full capability of this field is yet to be realized. It is exciting to be at the forefront of the journey.

What we do know is that this information is powerful and transformative. We have witnessed it thousands of times over, and have experienced it ourselves. It is always a buzz to see the light go on for people who can finally wrap their head around intangible things that have eluded them:

Why do I behave and think this way?
Why do I continue to do things I don't want to do?
Why am I so anxious and stressed?
Why do I care so much about what others think of me?
Why do I self-sabotage?
Why do I think and react irrationally?
Why am I so insecure?
Why do I resist compliance?
Why do I have trust issues?

And finally:

Why can't I change?

We are here to give you permission to give yourself a break. Give others a break. You are normal. You are designed this way for good reason. It's not you, it's your brain. We don't belabor this point to give you an excuse to continue partnering with unhelpful patterns of thinking and behavior. Quite the contrary. Acknowledgment of this fact, and ownership and acceptance of it, is your critical first step to change.

When you don't know what you don't know, you are powerless. It is impossible to change things that are not defined, or that you can't perceive or comprehend. It is much like roaming through life in the dark, devoid of your senses, and then blaming yourself or others when you inadvertently collide with them and injure yourself. Access to your senses gives you an awareness of yourself and your surroundings that enables you to navigate life more purposefully and successfully.

Think of SAFETY as another mode of sensory perception. In the same way that your physical senses are your guides to the physical world, consider SAFETY as your guide to the psychological world. Remember, your brain does not distinguish between the two when it comes to your safety.

Our hope is that this knowledge empowers you with keys to unlock the mental prisons that have held you back. Insights about yourself, your relationships, and your teams will serve to improve your world and theirs.

Recall that there are no losers with psychological safety. We envisage a world where workplaces and households are transformed into psychologically safe ecosystems, where the psychological safety of people and teams are nurtured, and where performance thrives.

We hope that you were able to find yourself in the stories. We hope that they reflected the ways you have experienced the world, whether personally or by observation. We encourage you not only to embrace SAFETY, but to identify additional ways to leverage it in your life and relationships.

SAFETY is a powerful way to bring out the best in yourself and others. In the words of Spiderman's Uncle Ben, "With great power comes great responsibility." Harness that power responsibly. It will help you create more meaningful interactions and allow you to enjoy richer and more productive experiences in all aspects of your life.

We look forward to hearing your stories.

BE SAFE ☺

BIBLIOGRAPHY

Ames, Daniel, Jenkins, Adriana, Banaji, Mahzarin, Mitchell, J.P. (2008). Taking Another Person's Perspective Increases Self-Referential Neural Processing. *Psychological Science*, 19, 642-644

Arnsten, Amy (2010). Stress Signalling Pathways That Impair Prefrontal Cortex Structure and Function. *Nat Rev Neurosci,* 10 (6), 410-422

Berkman, Elliot, Kahn, Lauren, Merchant, Junaid (2014). Training-Induced Changes in Inhibitory Control Network Activity. *Jour Neurosci,* 34 (1), 149-157

Burkland, Lisa, Eisenberger, Naomi, Lieberman, Matthew (2007). The Face of Rejection: Rejection Sensitivity Moderates Dorsal Anterior Cingulate Activity To Disapproving Facial Expressions. *Soc Neurosci,* 2 (3-4), 238-253

Cao, Y., Contreras-Huerta, L., McFadyen, J., Cunnington, R. (2015). Racial Bias in Response to Others' Pain is Reduced with Other-Race Contact. *Cortex,* 70, 68-78

Cheng, Xuemei, Zheng, Li, Li, Lin, Zheng, Yijie, Guo, Xiuyan, Yang, Guang (2017) Anterior Insula Signals Inequities in a Modified Ultimatum Game. *Neuroscience,* 348, 126-134

Cools, R and Esposito, M.D. (2011). Inverted-U Shaped Dopamine Actions on Human Working Memory and Cognitive Control. *Biol Psychiatry*, 69 (12), e113-e125

Davis, F., Neta, Maital, Kim, M., Moran, Joseph, Whalen, Paul (2016). Interpreting Ambiguous Social Cues in Unpredictable Contexts. *Soc Cog Aff Neurosci*, 775-782

Denny, Bryan, Inhoff, Marika, Zerubavel, Noam, Davachi, Lila, Ochsner, Kevin (2015). Getting Over It: Long-Lasting Effects of Emotion Regulation on Amygdala Response. *Psychol Sci*, 26 (9), 1377-1388

DeWall, Nathan, MacDonald, Geoff, Webster, Gregory, Masten, Carrie, L, Baumeister, Roy, F. et al. (2011). Acetaminophen Reduces Social Pain Behavioral and Neural Evidence. *Psychological Science*, 21, 931-937

Dudai, Y., Kami, A., Born, J. (2015). The Consolidation and Transformation of Memory. *Neuron*, 88

Duhigg, Charles (2016). What Google Learned From Its Quest to Build the Perfect Team. *New York Times*, Feb 25, 2016

Dunbar, R. (1998). The Social Brain Hypothesis. *Evolutionary Anthropology*, 178-190

Edmondson, Amy (1999). Psychological Safety and Learning Behavior in Work Teams. *Administrative Science Quarterly*, 44, 350-383

Eisenberger, Naomi (2012). The Neural Bases of Social Pain: Evidence for Shared Representations with Physical Pain. *Psychosom Med*, 74, 126-135

Goldin, Philippe, McRae, Kateri, Ramel, Wiveka, Gross, James (2008). The Neural Bases of Emotion Regulation: Reappraisal and Suppression of Negative Emotion. *Biol Psychiatry*, 63, 577-586

Gordon, E., Palmer, D.M., Liu, H., Rekshan, W., DeVarney, S. (2013). Online Cognitive Brain Training Associated with Measurable Improvements in Cognition and Emotional Wellbeing. *Technology and Innovation*, 15(1), 53-62

Holzel, Britta, Carmody, James, Evans, Karleyton, et al. (2010). Stress Reduction Correlates with Structural Changes in the Amygdala. *SCAN*, 5, 11-17

Hülsheger UR1, Alberts H.J., Feinholdt A., Lang J.W. (2013). Benefits of Mindfulness at Work: The Role of Mindfulness in Emotion Regulation, Emotional Exhaustion, and Job Satisfaction. *J Appl Psychol*, 98, 310-325

Jacobs, Tonya, Epel, Elissa, Lin, June, et al. (2011). Intensive Meditation Training, Immune Cell Telomerase Activity, and Psychological Mediators. *Psychoneuroendocrinology*, 36, 664-681

Koenigsberg, Harold, Fan, Jin, Ochsner, Kevin, et al. (2010). Neural Correlates of Using Distancing to Regulate Emotional Responses to Social Situations. *Neuropsychologia*, 48, 1813-1822

Kounios J1 and Beeman M. (2014). The Cognitive Neuroscience of Insight. *Annu Rev Psycho*, 93, 65-71

Krasner, Michael, Epstein, Ronald, Beckman, Howard, et al. (2009). Association of an Educational Program in Mindful Communication with Burnout, Empathy and Attitudes Among Primary Care Physicians. *JAMA*, 302, 1284-1293

Lieberman, Matthew, Eisenberger, Naomi, Crockett, Molly, et al. (2007). Putting Feelings Into Words Affect Labeling Disrupts Amygdala Activity in Response to Affective Stimuli. (2007). *Psycholgical Science*, 18, 421-428

Lieberman, Matthew (2013). *Social: Why Our Brains Are Wired to Connect*. Crown Publishers, New York

Lupien, S., Maheub, F., Tuca, M. et al. (2007). The Effects of Stress and Stress Hormones on Human Cognition: Implications for the Field of Brain and Cognition. *Brain and Cognition*, 65, 209-237

Mah, Linda, Szabuniewicz, Claudia, Fiocco, Alexandra (2016). Can Anxiety Damage the Brain? *Current Opinion in Psychiatry,* 29, 56–63

Marosi, Krisztina and Mattson, Mark, (2014). BDNF Mediates Adaptive Brain and Body Responses to Energetic Challenges. *Trends Endocrinol Metab*, 25, 89-98

Martin, Rebecca and Ochsner, Kevin (2016). The Neuroscience of Emotion Regulation Development: Implications for Education. *Curr Opin Behav Sci*, 10, 142-148

Mattson, Mark and Wan, Ruiqian (2005). Beneficial Effects of Intermittent Fasting and Caloric Restriction on the Cardiovascular and Cerebrovascular Systems. *Journ of Nutritional Biochemistry,* 16, 129-137

Mellman, T. A., Pigeon, W. R., Nowell, P. D., Nolan, B. (2007). Relationships Between REM Sleep Findings and PTSD Symptoms During the Early Aftermath of Trauma. *J Trauma Stress*, 20, 893-901

Mobbs, D., Meyer, M., Yu, R., Passamonti, L., Seymour, B.J., Calder A.J., Schweizer, S., Frith, C.D., Dalgleish, T. (2009). A Key Role for Similarity in Vicarious Reward. *Science*, 324, 900

Moran, J., Kelley, W., Heatherton, T. (2013). What Can the Organization of the Brain's Default Mode Network Tell Us About Self-Knowledge? *Front Hum Neurosci*, 7, 1-6

Muscatell, Keely and Eisenberger, Naomi (2012). A Social Neuroscience Perspective on Stress and Health. *Social and Personality Psychology Compass*, 6/12, 890-894

Nokia, Miriam, Lensu, Sanna, Ahtiainen, Juha, et al. (2016). Physical Exercise Increases Adult Hippocampal

Neurogenesis in Male Rats Provided It Is Aerobic and Sustained. *J Physiol*, 594.7, 1855-1873

Payne, Jessica and Nadel, Lynn (2016). Sleep Dreams and Memory Consolidation: The Role of the Stress Hormone Cortisol. *Sleep and Memory/Review*, 11, 671-678

Phan, K., Sekhar Sripada, Chandra, Angstadt, Mike, McCabe, Kevin (2010). Reputation for Reciprocity Engages the Brain Reward Center. *PNAS*, 107, 13099-13104

Stern, Stephen, Dhanda, Rahul, Hazuda, Helen (2009). Helplessness Predicts the Development of Hypertension in Older Mexican and European Americans. *Journal of Psychosomatic Research*, 67, 333-337

Stone, E. and Lin, Y. (2012). Open-Space Forced Swim Model of Depression for Mice. *Curr Protoc Neurosci.* January 1

Tabibnia G. and Lieberman M.D. (2007). Fairness and Cooperation are Rewarding: Evidence from Social Cognitive Neuroscience. *Ann NY Acad Sci*, 1118, 90-101

Tabibnia, G. and Radecki, D. (2018). Resilience Training That Can Change the Brain. *Consulting Psychology Journal: Practice and Research*, 70, 59-88

Weinstein, Galit, Beiser, Alexa, Hoan Choi, Seung, et al. (2014). Serum Brain-Derived Neurotrophic Factor and the Risk for Dementia: The Framingham Heart Study. *JAMA Neurol*, 71, 55-61

Wilson, T. D. (2002). *Strangers to Ourselves: Discovering the Adaptive Unconscious.* Cambridge, MA: Harvard University Press

Xu, Xiaojing, Zuo, Xiangyu, Wang, Xiaoying, Han, Shihui, (2009). Do You Feel My Pain? Racial Group Membership Modulates Empathic Neural Responses. *The Journal of Neuroscience*, 29, 8525-8529

Yee, Penny, Edmondson, Beverly, Santoro, Kristine, et al. (2007). Cognitive Effects ff Life Stress and Learned Helplessness. *Anxiety Stress and Coping*, 9, 301-319

Zamroziewicz, Marta and Barbey, Aron (2016). Nutritional Cognitive Neuroscience: Innovations for Healthy Brain Aging. *Frontiers in Neuroscience*, 10, 1-10

ABOUT THE AUTHORS

Dr Dan Radecki is Co-founder at the Academy of Brain-based Leadership (ABL) and serves as the Executive Director of CNS Research and Development at AbbVie Inc. Dan holds a Bachelors in Psychology, Masters in Biopsychology, and PhD in Neuroscience.

With his unique perspective from roles in both the leadership and neuroscientific worlds, in 2009 Dan created the content for the educational arm of the NeuroLeadership Institute and served as the lead professor and advisor for the Master of Science program in the Neuroscience of Leadership. This was the first university-accredited program ever developed to incorporate cutting edge neuro-science research into an optimal model of leadership. In the following seven years, Dan taught over 1000 leaders in 40 countries, on the neuroscientific underpinnings of effective leadership.

Dan has been published in scientific journals as well as the *Harvard Business Review*, delivered a TEDx keynote, and lectured internationally on topics such as the neuroscience of resilience, bias, creativity, leadership wisdom, the aging brain, the biology of collaboration, and the impact of stress on the brain. In his spare time, he can be found on the beautiful southern California coast with his wife Sara and three children, Alexis, Kyle, and Brendan.

Leonie Hull is Co-founder at the Academy of Brain-based Leadership (ABL) and has over 20 years' experience in management and consulting, predominantly in values based organizations.

In her previous role as General Manager of the Neuro-Leadership Institute (NLI), Leonie was instrumental in the formation, setup, and strategy of the organization. For over six years she operationalized and cultivated NLI's activities, team, faculty, and culture to build an internationally recognized platform and authority in the field of neuroleadership. It is here that her vision was birthed for a new approach to leadership, relationships, and how we do work.

ABL is as an extension and outworking of Leonie's passion to make a difference. Her personal vision is to create and facilitate pathways for individuals to more deeply know themselves and know others in order to create better lives, relationships, workplaces and communities.

She enjoys work and family life in Bondi Beach, Australia with her husband Craige and three children, Chaim, Lachlan, and Mikayla.

Jennifer McCusker sits on the advisory board for the Academy of Brain-based Leadership (ABL) and formerly served as the Senior Director, Global Talent and Organizational Development for Blizzard Entertainment.

Using a blend of creative and operational strengths, Jennifer has achieved career success through her no-non-sense business orientation. Jennifer has aided organizations across multiple industries in realizing their potential through people. Jennifer excels in performance and talent management, leadership development, and change management. In addition, she has uniquely positioned herself as an expert in integrating neuroscience research into her work. She has a passion for getting this research into the hands of our children and educators.

A Southern California native, Jennifer spends her free time making memories with her husband and daughter.

Christopher Ancona is an advisory board member for the Academy of Brain-based Leadership (ABL) and has spent many years on the forefront of the integration of neuroscience, social psychology, and biometrics into the training environment.

Beyond his passion for science-based learning, Chris is an internationally experienced engineering, project management, and change program professional with dual engineering and management education. His 17-plus years of experience span various industries such as automotive, education, and SaaS, and include launching technical greenfield projects, cross business unit project management, angel investing, and product development.

Chris spends time in Northern France with his partner Virginie and son Samuel, who together enjoy exploring the world.

ABOUT THE ACADEMY OF BRAIN-BASED LEADERSHIP

The Academy of Brain-based Leadership (ABL) consolidates and curates cutting-edge neuroscience research, products, training and assessments to address organizational transformation one brain at a time. Our practical and scalable solutions help workplaces support the wellbeing, safety and inclusion of its people.

From the individual, the team, to overall company culture—understanding the brain, managing its limitations, nurturing its needs and unlocking its resilience is key to optimizing potential and performance.

We maximize the impact of this new frontier in human development by creating powerful learning experiences designed to drive awareness, insight and action to empower sustainable change.